The College of West Anglia

Ramnoth Road • Wisbech •• PE13 2JE • Tel: (01945 582561)

Learning
Resource
Centre

The card holder is responsible for the return of this book
Fines will be charged on ALL late items

009158

Don Gresswell Ltd., London, N.21   Cat. No. 1208   DG 02242/71

IMAGES *of* CHILDHOOD
In Old Postcards

COLIN *&* TIM WARD

ALAN SUTTON

First published in the United Kingdom in 1991 by
Alan Sutton Publishing Limited · Phoenix Mill · Far Thrupp · Stroud · Gloucestershire

First published in the United States of America in 1991 by
Alan Sutton Publishing Inc. · Wolfeboro Falls · NH 03896–0848

British Library Cataloguing in Publication Data

Ward, Colin 1924–
Images of childhood in old postcards.
1. Childhood, history
I. Title II. Ward, Tim
305.2309

ISBN 0–86299–865–4

Library of Congress Cataloging in Publication Data applied for

Typeset in 11/13 Goudy.
Typesetting and origination by
Alan Sutton Publishing Limited.
Printed in Great Britain by
The Bath Press, Avon.

CONTENTS

ACKNOWLEDGEMENTS

The Ward cousins gratefully acknowledge the help and advice they have had from a host of enthusiasts, collectors and dealers in old picture postcards. They are especially indebted to Brian Lewis for the loan of twenty-one postcards from his collection. His help was invaluable for the section 'Working Children'.

They are also grateful to Brian Standish for the postcards reproduced at the bottom of p. 57 and top of p. 103, to Bradford Heritage Recording Unit for the picture at the bottom of p. 101, and to Hugh McKnight for the picture at the bottom of p. 103.

Acknowledgements are due to West Suffolk Newspapers Limited for the two press photographs reproduced on p. 183, and to Athena International for permission to reproduce the modern postcard from Caroline Arber's Country Childhood Collection on p. 184.

INTRODUCTION

For about forty years the postcard served the same purpose that the telephone does today. It was a cheap, very convenient and incredibly quick way of sending a message. Plain cards were first issued as a Post Office monopoly. Picture cards were legalized in Britain in 1894, more than twenty years after their first use in continental Europe. The earliest pictures were small, with the message on the same side and the address and stamp on the reverse. In 1902 the 'divided back' was allowed and the golden age of the picture postcard began.

Available everywhere, usually for one old halfpenny, or at most twopence for 'real photographic cards', until 1918 they cost only a ha'penny to send.[1] That year the doubling of the cost of the stamp, combined with the end of the First World War, halved the number of postcards sent. But the outstanding fact about the postcard years is the unbelievable speed of delivery. There were several collections and deliveries every day.

A card could be sent to the butcher in the morning requesting that a shoulder of lamb or a pound of sausages to be delivered for supper the same night; or one could ask to be met at the station from the 6.15 p.m. train. If you went on a journey you could instantly announce your safe arrival.

Naturally an industry arose to serve this boom in instant communication. National firms produced cards for sale everywhere. Local photographers, printers and artists, found a ready market for both 'real' photographs in the days when newspapers were not yet able to reproduce them, and, as printing techniques advanced, for lithographic and half-tone reproductions of their work. They bought ready-printed photographic cards and almost as a matter of course produced family photographs and local events in postcard form.

The picture postcard became *the* popular means of recording any scene or news item from fires and railway accidents to church outings and school parties, as well as the vehicle for universal sentiments and greetings.

Beyond these, what should the subject be? Obviously the first choice was topographical. Here we are at Beachy Head, or this is the High Street of Barrow-in-Furness. 'X' marks our room in the boarding-house at Rhyl. They went further. In the days before any new building development anywhere was seen as an environmental disaster, the local photographer was busy recording each new street or shopping parade. Plenty of prints would be bought by the new residents or shopkeepers. This explains the importance of old picture postcards to historians and archivists today. Every local history collection has its files of postcards, because nobody else thought it worth recording the opening of the new tram depot or the building of Mafeking Terrace and Alexandra Avenue.

Very early in postcard history, however, came cards with universal themes: flowers, animals, motherhood and, above all, childhood. The comic postcard also made an early appearance: the joke to be shared between the sender and the recipient. Jokes are a very clear indicator of changes in our sense of what is funny. Purchasers could choose from a wide selection the appropriate card for the person at the other end. Would this particular image appeal to that person's sense of humour? Would this or that innuendo offend or delight them? Even today, seventy-five years after the postcard's heyday, on the wall of any workplace you can see a collection of current postcards from colleagues on holiday. The picture postcard survives as a way of saying 'Yes, I'm still thinking of you'.

The actor W.C. Fields once remarked that 'anybody who hates children and dogs can't be all bad', and his rebuke can be seen as a caustic comment on the widespread sentimentalization of the universal experience of childhood. Attitudes do change, however, over the generations; Victorian ballads and pictures that used to be regarded as junk are now prized. The same thing is happening to old picture postcards of children, animals, flowers and domestic bliss. Today they are painstakingly imitated.

We all have a series of mental snapshots of those days; a vague impression derived from our grandparents or great-grandparents of an Edwardian Indian summer when the sun was always shining, brought to a devastating end by the First World War. A multitude of the boys in their sailor suits who lined up obediently for the photographer in 1907 were dead ten years later. At one level we have an 'upstairs, downstairs' picture of the country life of the aristocracy: the nursery the schoolroom, the rituals of entertaining, hunting and shooting, and the army of servants who maintained it all. At another level there is the huge middle class, similarly sustained by domestic service, with the same assumptions that the boys should be sent off to preparatory and public boarding schools, and just occasionally the girls too. After this come endless layers of clerks, small tradesmen and skilled craftsmen; families where the father is in regular work, affluent enough to take an annual holiday, or at least Bank Holiday visits to Blackpool or Brighton, and to take a part in the rituals of church and chapel, and to visit parks and pleasure-grounds.

Down at the bottom are the urban and rural poor. We certainly do need to be reminded, as the historian Peter Laslett told us, thinking about the years which were the heyday of the picture postcard, that:

> Englishmen in 1901 had to face the disconcerting fact that destitution was still an outstanding feature of fully industrialised society, with a working class perpetually liable to social and material degradation. More than half of all the children of working men were in this dreadful condition, which meant 40 per cent of all the children in the country. These were the scrawny, dirty, hungry, ragged, verminous boys and girls who were to grow up into the working class of twentieth-century England.[2]

It would be absurd to expect the picture postcard industry to reflect all these social facts. Possibly the poorest of people would choose the most idyllic pictures, while the wealthy might post images of ragged children in support of their favourite charity. People have their pride, and on the day when the photographer came to immortalize that year's leaving class at the elementary or junior school, perhaps the dresses and pinafores, boots, breeches or Eton collars were borrowed for the occasion.

Poor children were not alone in their exposure to privations and contagions. The children of the rich could die from tuberculosis or diphtheria too. The recollections of George Orwell and many others reveal squalor, discomfort and damp in those Spartan conditions that were thought to produce sturdy citizens.[3] It was Orwell, too, who evoked the idealized picture of the 'perfect symmetry' of ordinary working-class family life so often seen in the postcards of the time:

> Especially on winter evenings after tea, when the fire glows in the open range and dances mirrored in the steel fender, when Father, in shirtsleeves, sits in the rocking chair at one side of the fire, reading the racing finals, and Mother sits on the other with her sewing, and the children are happy with a pennorth of mint humbugs, and the dog lolls roasting himself on the rag mat.[4]

It is like one of those lovingly-composed tableaux in a folk museum, full of carefully assembled bygones and bits and pieces salvaged from demolished streets, but not really reflecting the poverty they purported to display.

This indoor life of the ordinary child is almost outside the range of the picture postcard except in staged studio pictures and the work of humorous artists, concentrating on family rows, bedtime and bathtime. Propagandists concerned with overcrowding and slums, or with the exploitation of child labour at home making matchboxes, Christmas crackers, buttons or brushes would issue postcards to publicize social evils. The commercial trade ignored the seamy side of life.

Children were everywhere in the street scene of Edwardian Britain, partly because families were larger and secondly because the years of schooling were shorter. Until the end of the First World War most children left school by the age of thirteen out of economic necessity; their income was vital for the family budget. Girls would join the army of domestic servants, boys would become errand or delivery lads, always visible in the streets, or 'learners' (as opposed to apprentices) in industry or retail trade, to be sacked at the moment when they became entitled to an adult wage.

Postcards accidently revealed another reason for the presence of children on the streets: it was a time when everyone enjoyed the freedom of the street. Before the surrender of the highway to the private motorist it was natural to pause for a conversation in the middle of the road, stepping out of the way of horse-drawn traffic and trams, and it was equally natural for children to play skipping games, hopscotch, football or cricket in the street, only grudgingly stepping aside to let the traffic through. Today few urban parents are happy at the thought of their children playing in the street, and most children with access to a bicycle are told by their parents not to use it in the street. It is a freedom that has had to be surrendered because of the revolution in transport.

There is a fourth reason why old picture postcards are full of children. Poor people, even as late as the Second World War, lived at population densities which now seem beyond belief. There were areas of Paddington with 400 people to the acre and in Glasgow with as many as 900 inhabitants to the acre. Children were doing the whole family a service by spending most of their waking hours outside the home. Whether the photographer wanted them or not, they were there.

In the years before radio and television, when even the cinema was in its infancy, the street itself was a theatre of drama and excitement. It was populated with peddlers, traders and hawkers. Old people fondly recall the muffin man, sellers of hot chestnuts or sherbert, the old-clothes man with his barrow, pony and bell, or the man exchanging goldfish for jam jars. When the organ-grinder brought his barrel organ and his monkey down the street, the girls would start dancing. When the man with his incredible dancing bear and his tambourine appeared, the children would form an awed circle around the poor chained beast. When the street fiddler or accordian-player arrived, the children would follow as though he was the Pied Piper.

Most people associate the postcard with the seaside. It is from here that many were posted. Even day-trippers, before the institution of holidays with pay, never failed to send cards to relations. Apart from comic cards with saucy jokes, there were instant pictures from the photographer on the promenade, and booths where the family poked their heads through a painted scene of boats, beaches, bi-planes or the Ghost Train. There were also ready-made themes, like shells, buckets-and-spades, sand-castles, bathing machines and Punch and Judy shows. Children were seen as natural subjects of the seaside postcard.

Advertisers were quick to recognize the usefulness of children. From the famous 'Bubbles' by Sir John Everett Millais, advertising Pear's Soap and the Mazawattee Tea scene of the little girl and her grandmother, down to the Bisto Kids, children had the same place in postcard advertising as they have in television commercials today. When Pear's produced paintings of girls aspiring to be ballerinas or curly-headed boys at the wicket, they were quickly followed by local photographers, who were not advertising soap. If charities produced pictures of tramps or destitute flower-sellers, the postcard producers dressed up children as ragged but jaunty vagabonds or charming barefoot waifs. They made poverty, which was an everyday background of Edwardian life, into something that was both cheerful and cheeky.

If a study is made of the cards produced in studios or by artists and cartoonists for the firms that distributed their work nationally, it is possible to argue that on many issues, visual anecdotes about children were a way of making adult experiences tolerable. The experiences of both world wars had to be insulated by turning them into a joke about children. During the period of long-term unemployment in industrial towns in the twenties and thirties, postcards were published showing one little boy asking another 'Are you working?' A postcard with the title 'One way of paying the rent' has a boy mounted on a stool, held fast by his sister, prizing open the cash box of the gas meter.

This moved a practice that was felt to be shameful yet necessary into the realms of comedy. With a daily shortage of small sums in ready cash, the meter was there as an instant and temporary source. Retribution would come when the gas man came to read the meter and empty the box. The universal borrowing among poor people was legitimized by giving it a comic setting in childhood escapades. What would be a stigma and disgrace in the adult world was simply a joke when projected on to children.

The other continual aspect of the lives of the poor was the pawnshop around the corner, symbolized by its sign of three brass balls. Household items, jewellery, bed-linen and the best suit, were pawned one week so as to have the money to buy food, in the hope that next week they could be redeemed. The tragedies and humiliations this situation produced can best be realized if you imagine yourself in those circumstances. It had to be made bearable by turning it into a joke, so there were comic cards of the children taking unlikely objects to the pawnshop: father's belt or the new baby.

As everyone was once a child and as most people become parents, we all have strong emotions about childhood. Funny cards project adult dilemmas into childhood, but at the other extreme was the idealization of childhood. The chocolate-box imagery of children brings derision today, although it survives in the world of birthday cards. It has even been suggested, within the world of postcard collectors that sometimes the motives of the publishers have to be questioned.[5] But the postcard industry censored itself, with exceptions like 'naughty' postcards from the seaside, of the Donald McGill kind, which very occasionally used children as innocent expressors of sexual sentiments. The pretty child was replaced by a different kind of carrier of adult humour: the cute child. In a long career as a postcard artist, Mabel Lucie Atwell produced cards for Valentine of Dundee from 1911 to 1964. She had, and still has, a great following. Other artists found it hard to escape her influence. But comic cards present a miniature social history of their own: that of the changing character of the British sense of humour.

Old postcards have been through the same cycle of valuation as old furniture or crockery. When Granny died, her possessions, being neither antique nor modern, were seen as tiresome old junk. Her prized postcard album might have been given to a grandchild, sold to a local dealer or put out for the dustman, or burnt. Old postcards went through the same metamorphosis as any other artefact. They were first dismissed as cheap and tatty junk. Then they became funny, amusing or quaint; visual evidence of the absurdity of an earlier generation. Only very slowly did they come to be seen as valuable collectable items.

Historians became interested in postcards as direct evidence of the past. And images of childhood gradually emerged as one of the most significant aspects of this historical legacy. As children are seldom free to make their own decisions, they reveal the way our predecessors expected children to behave, how they were dressed or undressed, their place in the economy, their education, their leisure both as arranged for them and as they made it themselves. All this evidence is filtered through the market that local or national postcard producers operated. But charitable organisations were there to present another side of childhood in order to arouse sympathy and support.

Today everything is different. Your local newsagent or stationer has local views of the High Street or the parish church, or national themes like royalty, the Trooping of the Colour or stars of television or popular music. The more direct and local aspects of childhood, along with other subjects are recorded personally, as most households possess a camera or video, or by local newspapers.

Now a totally different set of producers sell postcards. Museums and art galleries, including several museums of childhood, stately homes and heritage centres provide images to be kept as keepsakes or sent to friends. Specialist publishers bring reproductions of the work of painters and photographers who never managed, or never sought, to get taken up in the postcard market. Present-day children are dressed in modern versions of old-fashioned clothes to make new versions of old images.

The specialist collectors disdain all this, but it is obvious that in a hundred years time the old originals and the new simulations will merge into a generalized picture of the past. Future historians will probably regret that the adult version of the real or imaginary experience of childhood at the end of the twentieth century is not recorded with the same energy, diversity, accessibility and permanence that the postcard makers brought to its early years.

Chapter One

IN AND OUT OF THE STUDIO

Photography spread like wildfire in the second half of the nineteenth century. In its early decades it depended on 'messing about with chemicals' and consequently, apart from the band of enthusiastic amateurs, it began its connection that survives to this day with the local pharmacist's and chemist's shop. Ready-coated glass plates, chemicals for developing and printing, and factory-made photographic paper took the mystery out of photography, but by the turn of the century, just when the roll film and the box camera were beginning the democratization of the art, it was still a specialist occupation.

Today there are probably as many cameras as people in Britain, but in the early years of photography there were full-time or part-time professional photographers in every town and in many villages. Landscapes, buildings and places had to be recorded on location, but for portraits, just to reduce the exposure time and to control the lighting, the studio was the best location.

The new invention was seen as a godsend by the huge majority of the population: the people who could never dream of hiring a portrait artist, not even a fairground sketcher or itinerant silhouette-cutter to record what they looked like. Today we take it for granted that parents have some kind of photographic record of their children's growing years, fondly kept in an album or framed among the family bric-a-brac. The absence of such mementoes must have been keenly felt in the days of high child-death rates. 'Gone, and nothing to remember him by' is a phrase from Victorian tear-jerking melodramas that had real meaning.

The photographer's studio, whether in a booth at the fair or the seaside, or in the High Street or above the chemist's shop, met a universally-felt need. The *carte-de-visite* (3½ in by 2¼ in) was the standard size until the postcard replaced it.[1] Every local photographer could now buy in bulk ready-sensitized cards printed on the other side with a postal 'divided back'. They were used for every purpose: local views and events, and of course, the family photographs. Customers could buy a dozen and post them instantly to all their relations.

A more generous size demanded more in the way of props and backdrops in the studio, and following the tradition of British portrait-painting, scenery painted on canvas of country parkland, or of a great house or imposing room could be provided. At the seaside or the fair, the family could be photographed with their heads stuck through a coconut shy, or through the port-holes of a ship, or driving in a car or aeroplane. For children, going to the photographer's studio was an ordeal, like going the the dentist's. They had to wear their best clothes and to be on their best behaviour. The photographer might sometimes lessen the ordeal by producing fancy-dress or toys and rocking-horses, even real horses, stuffed for this purpose, or cricket-bats and wickets or baskets of dried flowers.

The firms that produced ready-made cards for as wide a market as possible knew that children, animals and flowers, or all three together, were subjects that appealed to purchasers for all occasions. Photographers assembled impossibly beautiful children, exquisitely-dressed, in poses that reflected an adult view of childhood. Who knows what agonies of embarrassment the child models suffered, dutifully kissing each other under the mistletoe or down by the old mill stream?

These idealized pictures from the postcard industry established the norm for portrait photographs of children. They were to be in the bath, fondling pets or listening to the canary in its cage, boys playing games or being soldiers, girls picking flowers or being nurses. Sometimes the results are touchingly different from the aim. Some girls never wanted to be milkmaids, some boys are unconvincing as angelic choristers. New photographic techniques enabled the photographer to wander the locality picturing children at their own front or back doors, knowing that Mother could not resist buying one print and would probably order several at a bargain rate to post to relations. At the seaside the roving photographer would take his candid camera everywhere, it could be a very profitable venture.

1:1

1:1 Studio portrait of a Liverpool family c. 1890. The children are beautifully dressed in velvet dresses and suits with lace collars and cuffs. The whole effect is negated by the father in his working suit and no tie. Browning, Barnes and Bell, Liverpool photograph.

1:2

1:2 The tradition of the static Victorian studio portrait lived on into the twentieth century. This little boy stares stolidly into the camera revealing, eighty years later, details of fashion for middle-class boys, *c.* 1912.

1:3 Another posed studio photograph of a brother and sister in their new winter coats. Both the girl's large hat and her doll's hat reflect the 1908 fashion for huge ladies' hats, often embellished with flowers and feathers. Anon. photograph. Posted Harleston, July 1908.

1:3

1:4

1:4 Stout boots were worn as a matter of course by most boys during the first half of this century. This young horseman was no exception. Anon. publisher.

1:5 Little Doris, a music-hall entertainer, stands in characteristic stage pose for a publicity postcard. Publicity cards were used in large numbers due to the low cost of both the cards and postage. Young children appeared regularly in music-hall acts in Victorian and Edwardian times. Publisher E. Pittingale, 72–74 Bark St., Bolton.

1:5

1:6

1:6 This young parlour maid poses in her new uniform for a photograph for the family album. Hours were long and time off short, so postcards were an easy way for a family to keep in touch and exchange gossip. Anon. publisher.

1:7

1:7 A really delightful study of a little girl, wearing her mother's hat and spectacles, cuddling the family cat. Anon. publisher. Posted July 1907.

1:8 This barefoot little boy is posed to look like his father relaxing after work, with glasses, newspaper, matches and pipe. Anon. series 1674.

1:8

1:9 In Edwardian days only wealthy families could afford a camera. Others who wanted family and children's photographs had to visit the local photographer for their mementoes. ·Studios were geared up for this demand with a variety of toys for use as props or accessories to keep the children happy and make the picture more 'natural'. Here Joan, aged 3½, of Edgbaston looks up from a precariously balanced doll's house for her portrait. Publisher Thornaby Bros., 21 Abbey Road, Bearwood, Birmingham. Posted June 1914.

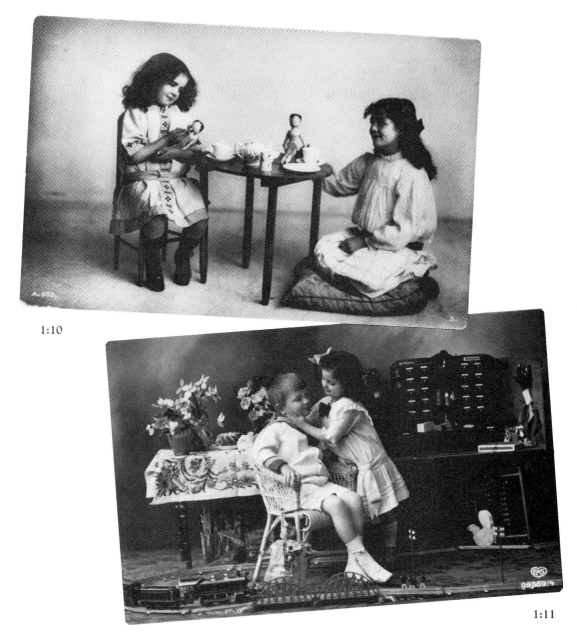

1:10

1:11

1:10 Two little girls pose prettily for the photographer during a dolls' tea party in a studio. Anon. Posted 31 December 1910.

1:11 Another pretty study of children playing with a variety of toys, which are valuable collector's items today. The toy shop on the table is a collector's dream, as is the model train. Note under the table a toy fort and also a large counting frame. Publisher Schwerdtlieger & Co., Berlin.

1:12 & 13 'Girls with flowers' was a popular theme, which the national publishers tackled with great expertise. **1:12** R. Tuck's 'Oillette', 'Flower Maidens', set 6966. Posted August 1908. **1:13** This very pretty girl posed for Raphael Tuck's 'Sunny Childhood' series S66. Posted 1903.

1:13

1:12

1:14

1:15

1:14 & 15 It was hard for local photographers in the studio . . . and even harder in the garden.

1:16

1:16–19 Boys and dogs were a favourite combination.

1:16 Published by Rotary Photo, London.

1:17 Published by Raphael Tuck.

1:17

1:18

1:19

1:18   Published by JWB of London.

1:19   Alpha Publishing Co.,
2/8 Scruton St., London. It must have
taken hours to capture this pose of both
child and dog. Posted 1930.

1:20

1:21

1:22

1:20 & 21   A rocking horse was an essential piece of studio equipment. **(1:20)** Anon. publisher. **(1:21)** Published by The One Studio, 49 Tottenham Court Road, London.

1:22   Alternatively, a *real*, if stuffed, horse and the appropriate clothing for cowboys . . . Published by Dura Ltd.

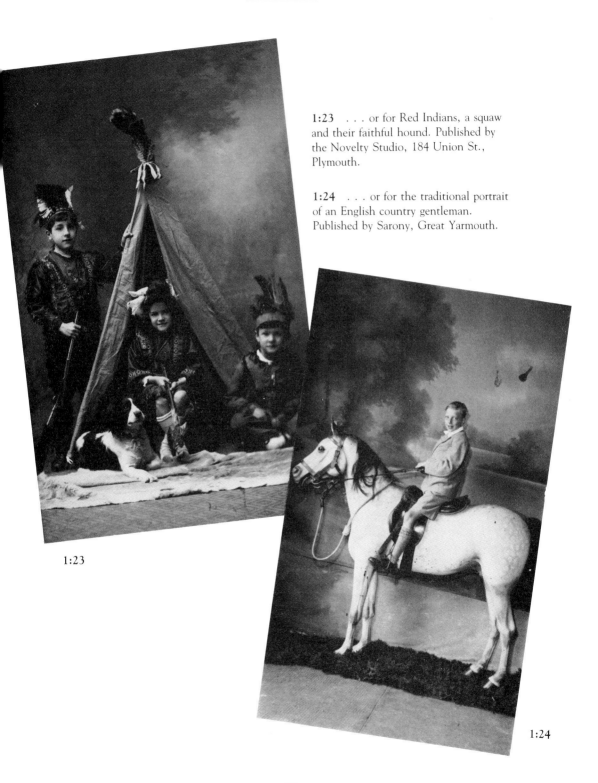

1:23 . . . or for Red Indians, a squaw and their faithful hound. Published by the Novelty Studio, 184 Union St., Plymouth.

1:24 . . . or for the traditional portrait of an English country gentleman. Published by Sarony, Great Yarmouth.

1:23

1:24

1:25

1:25 & 26 Gradually some postcard publishers moved out of the studio to make carefully posed images of domestic life. Despite being posed these cards are nevertheless very revealing in their details of everyday life, furniture, toys, clothes, etc.

1:26

"DOLLIE'S WASHING DAY."

"THE VILLAGE BLACKSMITH."
" And children coming home from school
Look in at the open door;
They love to see the flaming forge
And hear the bellows roar,
And catch the burning sparks that fly,
Like chaff, from a threshing floor."

1:27

1:27   Published by Valentines. Posted Dundee 1906.

1:28   Once out of the studio photographers discovered less romantic aspects of daily life. Here is pork for the neighbours for weeks. This scene was enacted throughout the country whenever a family's pig was killed. The local butcher (or his assistant) performed the task, helped by neighbours who shared the meat. Children helped too as a matter of course. The left-hand corner on this card was left blank for a message to the friend who was getting a gift of a pound of sausages.

1:28

25

1:29 A visit to the zoo, a subject th[at] was endlessly photographed. This card from 1920 is by Viner of Bristol and shows Clifton Zoo.

Rides on unusual animals was a favourite topic in and out of the studio.

1:30 & 31 An improbable ride with a pair of lambs in Edwardian days (1:30), and a real ride in a goat cart (1:31). Photographed by Chambers of Weymouth in the 1930s.

1:30

1:31

1:32

1:32–34 When trade was slack the local photographer would tour the back streets offering cheap postcards for the family album. The results were very different from his studio shots. This type of postcard was usually sold for 2d., which was a reasonable amount when wages were low and families were large. Ordinary printed postcards were ½d. each. These are typically posed shots revealing details which make so many photographic postcards historic documents, and accounts for their present popularity. These three postcards were anonymously published *c.* 1910.

1:33 A typical pose on the front steps. Boots were standard wear for poor children, while the little girl is wearing leather leggings. The steps were whitened at least once a week as a matter of family pride.

1:33

1:34

1:34 Younger sister's hand instinctively reaches out for reassurance as the photographer takes their photograph.

1:35 The English were famous for their passion for growing flowers, even in the smallest of urban backyards, but how careworn the parents look!

Chapter Two

PART OF THE SCENERY

Long before photography, artists had learned that human interest was an important ingredient of any scene. So it was as natural for the photographer as for the landscape artist to gather up the occupants of the street as part of the vista. In the early days the length of exposure required for a successful photograph demanded immobility. The height of summer, when the daylight was best, was the obvious time for taking pictures and, although adults would be at work in fields, factories or workshops, kitchen or wash-house, children were usually visible.

A guaranteed market had arisen for the postcards. If your own child was among those* immortalized in a scene, then even families who, just because of expense, would not have dreamed of taking little Bertie or Beattie to the photographer's were delighted when they were to be found on the local street scene card.

Years before the postcard era, a number of photographers, like Paul Martin in London, P.H. Emerson in Norfolk or Frank Sutcliffe in Whitby, had perfected the ways of incorporating children into their pictures, going about their normal activities in country and city. It took a long time for their work to enter the postcard market. Often the postcard makers would simply line up the available children across the road and tell them to stand still and smile. However, they learned quickly. The Chelmsford photographer Fred Spalding developed the technique of turning some kind of activity for the local children into an art. Travelling round Essex villages he would fill the empty street or green with girls skipping, or boys playing leapfrog at his command.

Not only this; when something extraordinary happened: a fire, a train crash, an accident, a riot or a trade union demonstration, children were always the first on the scene. When the local photographer arrived with his tripod to immortalize the event, he could be certain to find the children already there. 'I saw it happen, mister . . .' they would tell him and, within twenty-four hours, he would have postcards on sale to send to Auntie Flo. This was quicker than the local newspaper, which in those days very rarely included photographic pictures.

At the beginning of the nineteenth century Britain was a predominantly rural nation. Its children were country children. By the time it ended, and the postcard period began, it was a land with a majority of town dwellers. But old habits came to town. When the rose-grower, Harry Wheatcroft was a child every third family had an allotment, and in the First World War it could be claimed that 'for every five occupied houses throughout the two kingdoms there is one allotment.'[1]

When the postcard recorded picturesque country life, haymaking or harvest, it was impossible not to include children. They had to be there, helping. Clifford Hills, born in Great Bentley, Essex, in 1904, remembered his first job as a rook scarer. 'So mother used to pack up sandwiches, the usual bread and jam sandwiches, and it was a terrible long day from half past six in the morning, and on one occasion it was foggy, very foggy, and I was half afraid of being in the field, really I was.'[2] This was not the kind of aspect of childhood that postcards immortalize.

But they do recall children's tasks in sheep-shearing, pig-killing, or at an ox-roasting ceremony. At a different social level they are shown being introduced to the sports of hunting or shooting. When the photographer was there he provided all sorts of accidental historical evidence. Sometimes they reveal a world of adult assumptions about what children should be asked to do. For example, Clifford Hills recalled being employed for a 12-hour day, 'and I wasn't big enough to wield a big fork and knock this stuff about at the age of thirteen . . . he used to come along and swear at me awful for not keeping up . . . I had tears in my eyes many a time from that old man.'

The advantage of the outdoor photographer's camera was precisely the children's unpreparedness. For the school photo or the church outing, mothers would go to great lengths to ensure that they had decent boots, clean dresses or jackets and Eton collars. Clothes were borrowed for a smart turn-out. But the accidental record of daily life in Edwardian England often shows hungry children with bare feet and ill-fitting handed-down clothes. They became part of the scenery being recorded.

2:1

LONDON TYPES IN 1877: ITALIAN STREET MUSICIANS

Town Hall Square, Llansawel.

2:1 & 2 Long before the postcard age, the great Victorian photographers had perfected the art of getting natural poses in the street. But their pictures were not seen as worth sending through the post until many decades later. Local postcard producers would simply tell the children in the street to stand still and face the camera. The children of Llansawel pose in the town square for Williams the photographer from Llandeilo. Posted, Llansawel, September 1907.

2:3

Aberdare, The Square.

2:4

2:3 The children really did have the freedom of the street in Aberdare, Glamorgan, with not even a horse in sight. W.W.S. Derwent series 4365. Posted Aberdare, March 1910.

2:4 Children in Sutton Bonnington, Nottinghamshire seem to have enjoyed the same freedom. Carter No. 99. Posted 1916.

2:5

2:6

2:5 Photographers always had an eye open for sales, so the more local children (and adults) who could be spread across the road, the more sales of the card would be guaranteed. Over fifty people outside Kidwelly Post Office should have meant a profitable day's work. Anon. publisher. Posted Kidwelly 1904.

2:6 The Essex photographer Frederick Spalding (1858–1947) solved the problem of filling the foreground by posing the village boys in many of the hundreds of postcards he produced of Essex villages. He sold these cards (and photographs) in his shop in Chelmsford High Street. Here boys from Writtle play leapfrog in the street.

2:7

Sometimes the messages are as interesting as the cards.

2:7 *Dear Mother, Am sending you a photo taken during the water famine here, with Claude sitting on a pillar with his water jack in his hand. They are at the public water tap waiting their turn. Love from all.* Posted Bargoed, 11 August 1905.

2:8 This message is reproduced with all its spelling errors.

2:9 *Dear Annie, I am sending a photo of myself to you. I was quite unconscious of the man and the camera. I am sending one to Ivy.* Bilben of Poole took this charming study outside the library in Mont Street, c. 1908.

29

POST CARD

For inland Postage ONLY this space may now
be used for Communication

THE ADDRESS ONLY TO BE
WRITTEN HERE

A
half-penny
stamp
for inland
one penny
foreign.

Dear Mother we arrived home about Eleaven
I thought I'd write this we because you
might think we had gone on to Blackpool
We had a beautiful dinner cold meat
sause, current Bread & ketchup, pepper
and salt and cheued pears, and
Ink gravy so I think we have had
a very good dinner I fairly enjoyed it
from yours loving son George Maxwell

2:8

2:9

2:10

2:11

New and exciting vehicles were always a
source of interest.

2:10 Dorothy Levitt and her car were
the centre of attraction during the
Automobile Association small car trials
at Hereford c. 1910. Anon. photograph.

2:11 A group of boys wait for a ride on
this superb Wallace and Stevens steam
lorry. Anon. photograph.

2:12

2:13

2:12 Loaded coal trucks descending the incline pulled empties up to the colliery on a wire rope at Gwaun Cae Gurwen. Local lads watch their elders sort out the chaos after the rope broke on 12 September 1907. D. Jenkins the local photographer recorded the scene.

2:13 Local boys watch Clacton Fire Brigade quell a fire at Hollybush Hill, Great Bentley, Essex. The farmer's infant son had been playing with matches.

2:14

2:15

Industrial disputes had an immediate
impact on the lives of children.

2:14 Children on the fringe of a mass
meeting at Newport during the railway
strike of 1911. W.B. Bubby,
122a Chepstow Road, Newport.

2:15 Children queue for a meal at a soup
kitchen in Billeter Square, London during
the 1926 General Strike. Anon. publisher.

2:16 Children in the camp of evicted miners at Hemsworth, Yorkshire, August 1905. When the coal industry was privately owned, miners usually lived in colliery-owned houses. In a dispute over payments the Hemsworth Colliery Company refused to abide by an arbitration decision. The men came out on strike 'and they were successively evicted by warrant – some physically, others leaving of their own free will – from their houses. Great public sympathy was shown and many people visited the tented camp which was set up. The landlord of the Kinsley Hotel provided shelter for fifty-three of the children.' Postcards helped to win support for the evicted miners and their families.

2:17 Children and wives of Aberdare strikers taking home coal from the tips. Old Dyffryn Colliery, Cymbach.

2:16

2:17

2:18

2:19

2:18 An early coloured card in which the photographer has caught a tranquil detail of street life. National series.

2:19 What *can* be happening in this curious card from Whitehaven? Dalzell's series.

Chapter Three

THE SCHOOLCHILD

By the beginning of the picture postcard era schooling had long been 'free, compulsory and universal' as a result of the Education Acts of 1870 and 1886. The children of the affluent attended private schools, as they do to this day. It would be wrong, however, to conclude that until the State intervened, the children of the poor were illiterate. By the mid-1870s a quarter of working-class children attended privately-run schools. Recent historians have reassessed the history of Victorian education.[1] Many children in rural areas went to the schools run by the rival 'National' and 'British' societies, but as Ronald Blythe explains, 'There were many more village schools before the 1870s than is now popularly supposed, some of them offering eccentric and very interesting curricula as a charitable squire or loving clergyman brought in a graduate to give the parish children simple versions of the kind of education they'd had themselves . . .'[2]

As the official system developed, we can sometimes glimpse at the back of the group postcard, not a graduate, but a 'pupil-teacher' not much older than the children themselves, working her way into the teacher-training system. Until the age of thirteen children were required to produce a 'labour certificate' stating that they had reached a certain standard of education if they wished to be exempted from school. These were eagerly sought because the family often needed the child's earnings to supplement their income. It was often also a matter of pride for the family as well as of economic necessity. Summer and autumn were times of large-scale absence from school, and even saw farmers striding into the village school to demand that the children help with the harvest.[3] In some areas the term was adjusted to allow for the hop-picking season.

The most characteristic of all the souvenirs brought home from school and kept was the class photograph, taken in the playground and printed as a picture postcard by the local photographer. Its equivalent today is the coloured photograph of each individual child. Modern parents grumble but at one time in many British households the school postcard was the only visual record of childhood, therefore the tedious assemblage of fifty well-scrubbed faces lined up in the playground became a precious possession.

Internal scenes of school were not as universal, as they obliged the photographer to use magnesium flashlights and produced the dilemma of whether to present the teacher's view of the class – the ranks of attentive and well-behaved scholars sitting at their desks – or the class's view of the teacher, standing at a desk with the blackboard behind, seen across the cropped heads of the boys or the curls of the girls.

In the private sector everything was different. School proprietors used picture postcards to present not the pupils but the premises to potential parents. Here the emphasis was on the building, or the newly-equipped swimming pool, the chapel or library or the sporting achievements of the school and the military training offered. Even when children were taken to a photographer's studio, the appropriate props were seen to be a school desk or a big book to be studiously scanned with scholarly attention.

Informal postcards of school, or of playground activities are rare. However, with the broadening of the curriculum and the development of secondary education, cards depicted the new gymnasium that replaced drill in the hall, or the workshops, laboratories or domestic science room. Very occasionally school postcards contradict our stereotypes, and show boys learning to knit or to use the typewriter, or girl footballers.

Children themselves would often prefer to be somewhere else and the most characteristic comic cards of school are those which present cartoons of the bullying, begowned schoolmaster with a mortarboard, or the stern schoolmistress hectoring her little platoon of conscripts. It is, however, a view which is belied by many people's recollections of their schooldays, when teachers are recalled with affection.

The standard school photographs.

3:1 Best Sunday dresses and suits were
worn for the 1913 class photograph at
Burghill, near Hereford under the
watchful eye of schoolmaster Arthur
Bates. Anon. photograph.

3:2 'Sit straight and fold your arms
behind your backs!' Note the small
counting frames on the polished desk
tops and compare this with today's
informal classroom arrangements.

3:1

3:2

3:3

DORSTONE VILLAGE.

3:4

20371 Children coming home from school.

3:3 & 4 The photographer would sometimes catch the children coming out of school, either formally as (**3:3**) at Dorstone, Herefordshire, or informally (**3:4**). Wrench series 20371. Posted Dorstone, August 1915.

3:5

CARTMEL FELL SCHOOL

CORNISH SCHOOL BOYS WITH THEIR PASTIES MID DAY MEAL

3:6

3:5 Everyone's idea of the village school. On examination you will see that it is carefully posed. In the foreground is a decorous boys versus girls tug-of-war. Beyond, boys are practising the Cumberland style of wrestling, and in the background, the ubiquitous ring-a-ring-of-roses. Renshaw series.

3:6 Four working-class lads dressed like their fathers in boots, leggings, caps and jackets buttoned up against the cold eat the traditional Cornish pasty lunch. J.E. Oatey, Wadebridge.

3:7

3:8

MAIDSTONE VIOLIN CLASS (BOYS), HATHERSHAW BOARD SCHOOLS, OLDHAM.

Music-making, then as now, was highly valued.

3:7 A team of schoolboy carol singers and the sum they had earned for charity. W. Rooke, 37 Pelham Road, South Gravesend.

3:8 A large class of fiddlers. Gale & Polden, Wellington series.

3:9

3:10

3:9 There is still a tradition of children's marching bands in South Wales. Here Fleur de Lys Infant's Band, Monmouthshire, pose outside their school. With their assorted drums, tambourines, whistles, triangles, rattles, etc the sound can only be imagined! Anon. publisher.

3:10 Informal music in the street. Children with home-made drums in the streets of Aberfan c. 1930. Anon.

3:11

St.Elizabeth's House Bullingham – Drill

3:12

3:11 Convent girls drill in the playground at St Elizabeth's House, Bullingham in the 1920s in this promotional postcard. Sets of such postcards were issued by many private schools at this time. Published by P.A. Buchanan & Co., Croydon, Surrey.

3:12 Typing class for the boys at Taunton Grammar School. Anon.

3:13 & 14   The new High Schools and
the old Public schools were proud of
their facilities for practical learning, such
as laboratories and workshops. **3:13**
Publisher, H. Palmer, Ross on Wye.
3:14 P.C. Hunt, Paternoster House,
London, No. 24335.

3:13

3:14

THE CARPENTER'S SHOP, ST. PAUL'S SCHOOL. W

3:15

3:15 & 16   For the artists of comic cards, teacher was usually the butt of jokes about school. **3:15** Was posted *during raids* the sender says, on 21 December 1917. Artist, F.G. Lewis. Published by E. Hack. **3:16** Published by Bamforth. The old ones are still the best!

" Please Teacher I've lost my indiarubber."
" Well, use the little boy's behind."

BLIND MAN'S BUFF.
"I KNOW—IT'S TEACHER!"

3:16

Chapter Four

FUN AND GAMES

Until the motor car turned the street into a lethal place for children, the street was the centre of children's games. Old postcards reinforce the evidence of historians that 'young children used to stretch their skipping ropes right across the main street from one cottage door to another. Not until 1914 was it suggested in the school minutes that playing in the road might be dangerous.'[1] The picture postcard arrived on the scene in time to record outdoor games like conkers, bowling hoops and spinning tops, skipping, leapfrog and hopscotch, and those endless running and chasing games.

But even before the advent of the postcard and the motor vehicle, studies of children's play assumed that traditional games were dying out. In 1894, introducing her collection of *Children's Singing Games*, Alice Gomme remarked that 'When one considers the conditions under which child-life exists in the courts of London and of other great cities, it is almost impossible to estimate too highly the influence which these games have for good on town-bred populations' and she regretted that 'it is one of the misfortunes of present-day society that our children lose the influences from the natural playing of games.'[2] The writer Norman Douglas accumulated his collection of *London Street Games* in 1916, and when it was reprinted in 1931 he asked, 'I wonder how many of these games are still played?'[3] However, when Iona and Peter Opie published their book *Children's Games in Street and Playground* in 1969, they reminded us that this belief in the decline of traditional games is itself a tradition, and they cite a series of famous authors like H.E. Bates, J.B. Priestley, Richard Church and Howard Spring as falling victims to the assumption. They were bold enough to give us lists of those street games which really are diminishing and those which are growing in popularity. They found a marked decrease in the popularity of games which victimize one player and an increase in those in which children compete on equal terms, a decrease in the ones which are most promoted by adults, and a continued flourishing of those which adults themselves are least likely to play well, or are likely to encourage. They found that, when free of adult organization, games were, according to your viewpoint, often extraordinarily naive or highly civilized. 'They seldom need an umpire, they rarely trouble to keep scores, little significance is attached to who wins or loses, they do not require the stimulus of prizes, it does not seem to worry them if a game is not finished.'[4]

Playground and playing-field had to replace the street as the place for play and, paradoxically, the twentieth-century outdoor activities that are well-recorded on postcards are individual activities on wheels: roller skates, scooters, fairy cycles and toy cars, or go-carts made from orange-boxes and old pram wheels.

The postcard-makers concentrated on those games which were obvious to the outside observer, like blind man's buff, ring-a-ring-of -roses, kissing under the mistletoe or on St Valentine's Day. In the nineteenth century, something new had entered British life: organized team games, intended to civilize traditional football or cricket. They spread from the boarding schools of the rich to ordinary schools and to every local group in town and village. Gymnastics and athletics were expected to build a healthier nation. 'Sports days' were added to the programme of country fairs and to the end-of-year celebrations in schools. The winning teams in every competitive sport and game were photographed with their prizes.

4:2

4:1

4:1 & 2   Two faded, small size postcard pictures showing a game of marbles and an early form of roller skates. Anon.

4:3

4:4

Ring a Ring o' Roses

4:3 & 4 Ring-a-ring-of-roses was one of
the few children's games that the
postcard makers understood and endlessly
illustrated. The game is a folk memory
from the great plague of the Middle
Ages. **4:3** It is played on a village green
in Kent. Published by Photochrome Co.,
London, No. 236. Posted May 1903. **4:4**
Set up in the studio. Published by J.W.
Bland, 122 Commercial Road, London.

"Familiar Figures of London"   Copyright.

No. 8. — The Street Organ.

4:5

4:5 & 6   Servant girls (**4:5**) and schoolgirls (**4:6**), dance in the street to the music of the barrel-organ. Before the days of electrical amplification of records, or of radio, this was the most commonly heard music in public places and the organ-grinder would buy or hire a repertoire of current popular songs. The message on **4:5** refers to peace with the Boers and to the competition, run by Tucks, for the biggest collection of their postcards. Posted June 1902. **4:6** Published by Star series, Gottschalk, Dreyfus & Davis, London. Posted October 1906.

DANCING TO ORGAN.   Copyright.

4:7

4:8

Boys, but not girls, claimed the right to
bathe in the river or pond in summer
time. Although costumes were not
thought to be necessary, the
photographer would paint them on.

4:7 Swimming at Caerphilly,
25 August 1908.

4:8 'Water rats at play' in the River
Avon at Evesham. Published by Royal
Standard Publishing Co., Evesham.

4:9–11 Edward Patrick Kinsella was an Irish artist whose caricatures of sporting children were immensely popular. First published by Langsdorff and Co., London in 1907, they sold in vast numbers and became known as 'Kinsella Kids'. **4:10** Posted from Ledbury, 9 December 1909.

4:9

4:10

4:11

4:11 Another 'Kinsella Kid'. These postcards have a universal appeal and still retain their popularity.

4:12

4:12   Blind Man's Buff was another
regular theme for the postcard artist.
Published by R. Tuck, Continental series
4104. Undivided back. Posted February
1903.

59

4:13

In real life, children were seldom as fanatical about their games as the 'Kinsella Kids'.

4:13   A young batsman faces up to an imaginary bowler in 1910. Anon.

4:14   A girls' game of cricket in 1907. Published by IXL.

A TEST MATCH.

4:14

4:15

BLOWING BUBBLES. "I'LL SHEW YOU HOW."

4:15 Blowing bubbles was a peaceful pastime depicted on this card from the Regent Glossy series. Posted in 1910.

4:16 A football match on England's largest village green, at Great Bentley, Essex, and two boys have simply lost interest and are having a wrestling match of their own. Posted February 1919.

A FOOTBALL MATCH ON GREAT BENTLEY GR

4:16

4:17

Wheeled playthings were enormously popular.

4:17   This girl and her scooter were photographed with a very inappropriate studio backcloth.

4:18   This girl with her tricycle was on her home ground. Anon.

4:18

4:19

4:19 Most popular of all was the home-made barrow or go-cart, which anyone could put together from an old wooden box and some pram wheels. This boy is allowing a younger child to 'drive'. Anon.

4:20 This little girl is entertaining the babies in a home-made 'dilly'. Anon.

4:20

4:21

4:22

4:21 Lord and Lady Davies of Llandinam used this family photograph as a Christmas card in 1932. Here they pose with their gun dogs and a brace of pheasants after a shoot.

4:22 A little boy carries his staff ready to join the hunt with his elders as the Hawkstone Otterhounds cast for a scent in a river in mid-Wales. Otter hunting is now illegal, of course.

Chapter Five

ORGANIZING CHILDREN

The freedom of the street was exactly what children found most alluring, but it was not a freedom that parents wanted for their children. Girls were far more strictly chaperoned than boys, and were kept at home by domestic tasks which were not so frequently demanded of their brothers. Although it was feared that boys would 'get into mischief' or into 'bad company', when they did, their elders were prone to reflect that 'boys will be boys', a sentiment endlessly echoed in comic postcards.

In 1883 a Glasgow business man, William Smith, fell under the influence of a revivalist preacher, George Reith of Hillhead (the father of the first director-general of the BBC), and sought to combine his experience as a member of the 1st Lanarkshire Rifles with his wisdom as a Sunday school teacher in the Free Church of Scotland. One of his admirers, Henry Drummond, wrote, 'Amazing and preposterous illusion! Call these boys "boys" which they are, and ask them to sit up in a Sunday class and no power on earth will make them do it; but put a fivepenny cap on them and call them soldiers, which they are not, and you can order them about till midnight.'[1] Thus began the Boys' Brigade.

The movement Smith began was highly successful. Its characteristic sound of bugles and drums was instantly recognizable, as was the uniform of pill-box hat and white belt. Parades, drill with dummy rifles and camps were a ready postcard subject, as were its many imitators from other religious demoninations, like the Church Lads' Brigade and the Boys' Life Brigade. When Baden-Powell wrote *Scouting for Boys* in fortnightly parts in 1908, it attracted a spontaneous audience of boys, some of them members of the Boys' Brigade, who formed their own troops before the Scout Association was officially founded.

By 1909 at least six thousand girls had become Boy Scouts, and at a rally at the Crystal Palace that year plenty of them turned up in their Scout hats and scarves, carrying their staves. Baden-Powell noticed them there and deputed his sister Agnes to hive them off at once into the body that became the Girl Guides. The new organization, however, was slow to grow, particularly as the girls' equivalent of Cubs were Rosebuds, only later redesignated as Brownies and perhaps the very activities which had encouraged the girls to join the Scouts were missing from the Guides. Eighty years later, in 1990, the Scout Association announced its decision to re-admit girls.

The intervening years saw an endless harvest of postcards of organized children in uniform, the Boys' Brigade, the Girls' Life Brigade, Scouts, Guides, Cubs and Brownies, church choirs, the Cadet Corps, gymnastic displays, cricket, football, hockey, lacrosse and swimming teams. As with school group photographs, they usually have the front row sitting, displaying cups or prizes, and the adult officers standing at the rear. There was the same guaranteeed market of proud parents and grand-parents who would buy the card. Enlarged versions could be framed and hung on the wall.

Very occasionally the photographs would capture pictures of indi-vidual children or small groups actually involved in some activity, and the viewer is able to catch the excitement or boredom, effort or apprehension on particular faces, usually lost in the crowd. The historians of this century of childhood report that:

> Most of these uniformed organisations achieved massive recruiting figures. In the 1930s the membership of the Boy Scouts rose to its highest ever level of almost half a million boys aged between ten and nineteen, while the Boys' Brigade boasted 150,000 members. In all, more than one in three British children passed through the ranks of one of these organisations during the inter-war years . . . They rarely reached the children of the very poor, or the 'hooligan' boys, as pioneers like Baden-Powell had dreamed. Many simply could not afford the uniform or were put off by the discipline and militarism. More important, if they did join it was often to be in the band or to go to the annual camp.[2]

They quote the derisive rhymes sung by the recruits who did not take seriously the discipline and patriotic propaganda that infused the organization of childhood. In the 1900s, children sang:

> 'Ere comes the Boys' Brigade,
> All smovered in marmalade,
> A tuppeny 'a'penny pill box,
> An' 'alf a yard of braid

Comic postcard artists enjoyed parodying the pitfalls of camping and outdoor life, but stopped short of ridiculing the founders' aims. The general impression is that the adult world felt more at ease when its children were organized. It was a matter of keeping them off the streets.

5:1

5:2

5:1 Smart uniforms and camping may not go well together, but that was what the leaders expected from the Boys' Brigade. Anon.

5:2 Despite their stiff uniforms and caps a group of GPO telegraph boys enjoy a weekend camp. Anon. publisher.

5:3

5:4

Ledbury Church Lads' Brigade.   *Inspection at The Holt, August 19th, 1909.*

5:3 The Boys' Life Brigade was founded in 1899 by a Congregational minister as an alternative organization without 'the least tincture of militarism'. Here the boys of the Oldham Brigade are shown with their leaders. Anon.

5:4 The Church Lads' Brigade was founded in 1891 with the intention of being *more* military than the Boys' Brigade. J. Tilley photographed the Ledbury Church Lads in 1909.

The Boy Scouts were founded in 1908 as a result of the huge readership of Baden-Powell's *Scouting for Boys*. The emphasis was on woodcraft and the appeal was to the 'natural boy', or so the founders hoped.

5:5 An unknown scout troop march off to camp pulling all their camping gear in a cart. Anon.

5:6 The local Ledbury troop cook a meal over a smoky fire at Bosbury. Published by Tilley, c. 1910.

5:5

5:6

5:7

THE BOY SCOUTS: Guarding an approach.

5:8

5:7 Scouting developed a similarity to military manouevres, and there were breakaway organizations, with names like the Brotherhood of British Boy Scouts, or Kibbo Kift, the Woodcraft Kindred. Published by Davidson Bros., London.

5:8 A group of young Morris dancers from the Manchester area pose for an anonymous photographer. The message on the back includes the words and music of the 'Lancashire Morris Dance'. The sender also requests *don't forget to bring (1) The Ludlow Ordnance Map (2) Haywards Botany (3) The Bernard Shaw books*. Posted Whittington 1909.

5:10

Baden-Powell rejected the idea of girls being part of the Scouts and deputed to his sister the task of hiving them off into the Girl Guides, which were founded in 1910.

5:9   A group of Guide leaders resplendent in uniform. Anon. publisher.

5:10   A typical Guide group, with the under-elevens as Brownies (known as 'Rosebuds' until 1914). Anon. publisher.

5:11

5:12

5:11 & 12 Sometimes, among all the postcards of parades and uniforms, we catch a glimpse of real children, like the Bicester Brownies (**5:11**) in 1928 (published by Harris Morgan, Market Square, Bicester), or the unknown troop of Scouts in camp (**5:12**).

Chapter Six

WAR AND THE CHILD

Playing at soldiers has, until recent years, been an approved activity for boys, and in the mid-nineteenth century the horrors of the Crimean War, when more soldiers died from diseases like cholera, dysentery and diarrhoea than were killed by the enemy, led to the cult of the great hospital reformer, Florence Nightingale, who reduced the hospital death rate from 42 per cent to 2 per cent. She, and the nursing tradition she founded, lived on into the postcard era, and nursing was seen as a worthy aspiration for little girls.

Having played at being involved in war as small children, they were enrolled into youth organizations with an unmistakably military emphasis. This was later denied, but the evidence of picture postcards is unmistakable. When war actually came, postcards had to relieve its disasters with an attempt at humour. Pictures of children were a means of insulating people from realities that were too hard to bear. In both wars children were dressed in military or nursing uniform, and photographed in various warlike situations by all the countries involved, as emulators of adults.

Both world wars had similarly to be treated with an attempt at humour. All wars of the pre-postcard era involved, apart from patriotic sentiment, a small proportion of the population: the wives and families of members of the fighting services. Twentieth-century wars were different in scale and scope as a result of conscription. It was the century of total war, and children were affected as never before, firstly by the scale of military casualties in the first war and then by evacuation in the second. Between the 1 and 4 September 1939, 1½ million people, mostly unaccompanied children in school parties, left British cities for unknown rural destinations. The sociologist John Macnicol uncovered a very significant fact about the Second World War in Britain: 'In 1939 less than half the population left home even for a single night of the year; yet during the course of the war there were 60 million changes of address in a

civilian population of 38 million.'[1] Faced with such large-scale disrup-
tions postcards turned to humour in an effort to minimize the effects of
war.

Both wars produced a postcard boom, though during the Second
World War it was on a far smaller scale because of the development of
other means of communication: the telephone or air letters for example.
But as the war involved civilians as well as service personnel, the
postcard remained the simplest way of sending a message when vast
numbers of people, including children, needed to tell family and friends
that they had arrived safely, where they were, and to ask after the other
kids, the neighbours and the cats and dogs.

Postcard artists turned the horrors and deprivations into jokes. We
have confined ourselves here to the First World War, as the same jokes
were recycled, sometimes by the same artists like Donald McGill and Reg
Maurice, in 1939–45.

6:1

6:1 Pembridge Volunteers. The local
schoolboys dress up as soldiers for a
village fête *c.* 1906, reflecting the
militarism and patriotism prevalent in
the years after the victory over the Boers.
Anon.

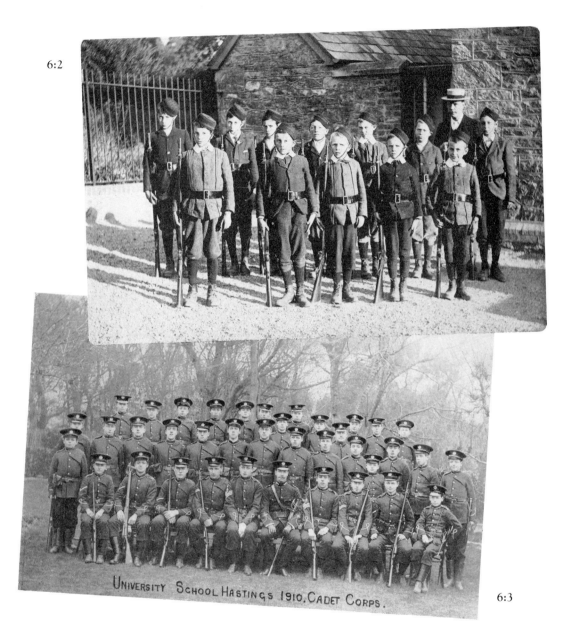

6:2

6:3

6:2 The Boys' Brigade in a Devonshire village parades for Mr Gay the local photographer, c. 1908.

6:3 All the best schools for boys had a Cadet Corps. Photograph by Bloomfield of Hastings, 1910.

6:5

Feine Nummer!
Wenn das der Vater müsste!

JEUNE.

Dressing up as a soldier like Dad is a universal desire mirrored by these three postcards.

6:4 A Parisian boy on his father's white horse.

6:5 A German boy is encouraged to smoke to copy his father even more.

6:4

6:6

6:6   This little boy with the gun and
rifle was photographed in Woodward's
studio in Guernsey.

6:7   In this studio picture the wounded
soldier is a girl the nurse a boy, preparing
for a fancy dress competition. Photograph
by Grave, Holsworthy.

6:7

6:8

6:9

6:8   A recruiting drive in 1916. The appalling losses on the Western Front brought about the introduction of conscription. Published by Silk & Terry, Birmingham. Posted Oxford 1915.

6:9   'Present and Future National Reserves' is the ominous caption for this patriotic card. Anon.

6:10   A little girl practices her nursing skills on the pet dog. Anon. publisher.

6:11 & 12   Turning the war into a joke. **6:11** Published by Inter Art Co., 'Kute Kiddies' No. 611. **6:12** Published by Bamforth Comics, series 507. Posted 1919.

6:10

6:11

6:12

6:13

MOTHER·· NOW YOU CHILDREN
SHUT UP.
BIG SISTER·· YES CHUCK IT YOUNG
ERB YOU'RE ONLY 'ARF
A BLOOMIN COUPON.

6:13 & 14   In 1914 Britain was heavily dependent on imported food as farmers could not compete with cheap imports. Rationing was introduced too late and, because of huge losses of shipping, the country was brought close to starvation in 1917. The cartoonists had to make light of it. **6:13** H.B. series, No. 1210. **6:14** R. Tuck & Son, 'Oillette', 'Curly Locks on short rations'. No. 3128.

6:14

6:15   In autumn of 1918 children of Great Bentley, Essex, picked 2½ tons o' blackberries. Photograph by D.N. Went Great Bentley.

6:15

6:16

6:17

6:16 & 17 Conscription too, had to be
treated in a way which concealed real
feelings. **6:16** H.B. series 1245.
6:17 Regent Publishing Co., 3143.

6:18

6:18 Paradoxically, real emotions and fears were expressed in a sentimentalized way. Philip Boileau was an American artist in the glamour market before the First World War. He produced a 'Patriotic' series, anticipating America's entry into the war, which was, however, printed and sold in Britain.

"THE COMING STORM"

Painted by Philip Boileau

6:19 When the war was over, temporary war memorials were erected, later to be replaced by the ones to be seen in every town and village. This card was published to commemorate a children's Christmas treat for war orphans.

COMRADES OF THE GREAT WAR (WOOLWICH AND DISTRICT BRANCH) CHILDREN'S XMAS TREAT.

The Glorious Dead

A CHILD'S TRIBUTE TO DEAR DADDY
YOUR TRIBUTE TO THE CHILD.

6:19

Chapter Seven

WORKING CHILDREN

Poor children – that is to say the majority of children – started work early, despite the Factories and Workshops Act of 1901 and the Education Act of 1902, which between them set the school-leaving age at twelve and forbade the employment of children under that age in factories.

To increase the family income boys had delivery jobs both before and after school. 'Every boy endeavoured to get a milk round because one of the great things of being a milk boy was that the milkman always used to give you a half a pint a day, which was a great asset to your family.'[1] This entailed starting at 4.30 a.m., leaving the milkman at 6.30 a.m., going home for a wash and a cup of tea, then a paper round until 8.00 a.m. in time for breakfast and to get ready for school. After school this boy delivered wallpaper and paint on a hand-cart for a builders' merchant. He was not yet in his teens.

The opportunities for girls to be employed in this manner were fewer. Country girls would leave home at thirteen or fourteen to join the army of one-and-a-half to two million domestic servants. Postcards do not reveal the endless drudgery of the housemaid's life, 'after a fourteen-hour day of cleaning floors and grates and boots, serving meals, making beds, answering the door, continually answering bells rung by the family for more water in their bedrooms, more coal and so on.'[2] Postcard artists tended to show domestic servants as older than they actually were. Or else they illustrate little girls acting out this role. For most housemaids the escape from life 'in service' was marriage, for which it was seen to be an appropriate preparation.

The firms producing postcards preferred to record cheerful children who had direct contact with the public in the street. Several of them issued series of cards illustrating topics like 'London Street Life', showing the bright and chirpy newsboy, the district messenger boy or telegraph boy on the doorstep, or the errand boy bringing the evening meal.

Usually when a girl is shown she is a flowergirl, sometimes with a younger child in tow. There are a few postcards which display these children as wistful, pathetic or vulnerable. Most of them were in what used to be called 'dead end jobs'.

There was another aspect of child labour which was handled delicately by the postcard maker. In 1907 there were 2,088,932 horses in the United Kingdom, each of them producing about forty-five pounds of dung daily. One of the nightmares of the pre-motor age city was that of cleaning the streets. Hence that institution of Victorian cities: the crossing-sweeper. Renamed the 'Orderly Boy' he appears on postcards, which also record the fact that the coming of motor vehicles brought a loss of income for the boys who could sell horse manure to gardeners at a ha'penny a bucket in the early years of the century, or a penny by the 1930s.

Most child labour was out of the public eye. But when the local photographer made a record of the factory or foundry, the spinning or weaving mill or the colliery upon which the local economy depended, we notice that some of the workers were very young indeed. Often it is only the recording on postcards of coal-mine or factory accidents that provide a reminder of the age at which children were introduced to long hours of exhausting and often dangerous work. They are certainly prominent in pictures of strikes, lock-outs, demonstrations and evictions from employer-owned housing. Children played an important part in the industry.

Pamela Horn records the experience of 'half-timers' employed in Lancashire cotton mills and Yorkshire woollen mills from the age of ten. 'Like other half-timers, Ben began to work at 6 a.m. and continued until 12.30 p.m. with a half-hour break for breakfast. "We then had to go to school from 2 to 4.30 p.m." The next week he went to school from 9 a.m. until 12 noon, and to work from 1.30 p.m. until 6 p.m.'[3]

It was not until 1936, that the proposal to raise the school leaving age from fourteen to fifteen was debated in parliament; yet Lord Halifax declared that manufacturers had assured him that there was work for nimble little fingers in the cotton mills of Lancashire. It should be remembered that many boys and girls of the picture postcard years felt that they should be at work contributing something to the household budget rather than staying on at school and remaining a financial burden to their families. Occasionally the postcards reveal the degree to which child labour was still, long after the industrial revolution when pauper children were sold to factories, an important aspect of Britain's industrial pre-eminence.

7:2

7:1 & 2 In the country it was always taken for granted that children needed to work. **7:1** The girl is feeding the (free range) chickens. But it was also true that women and children were employed on ill-paid tasks like stone-picking. They were used in spring time to gather stones in hayfields, so that the surface would be free of them when scything began.
7:2 Stone-gatherers at Fron Gabedj Farm, near Llandyssel, Dyfed, in 1890. Published by W. Evans, Spring Croft, Llandyssel.

7:3

7:4

Trussing Hay for Market.

29. 2. 04

The Wrench Series, No. 6814

7:3 Hay time and harvest were the seasons of the year which produced almost continuous hard work. Here boys help with the last load of hay near Bromley.

7:4 Before balers became commonplace, hay was trussed for market by the laborious process shown here. Hay was cut from the stack into 3 ft squares, then placed in a press, and compressed by the ratchet lever on the right. The young lad is attending to the string ties. Postcard by Wrench of London, published in 1903.

7:5 Sheep-shearing was always a busy time on a farm. The girl in white, turning the handle for the clippers, was doing a job usually done by a boy, while the girl in the centre is stacking the rolled fleeces. Anon. publisher.

7:6 Advertisement card for Burman sheep-shearers showing how cheap man (or even cheaper boy) power was utilized for sheep-shearing before the days of electric power on the farm.

7:5

7:6

7:7

THE
BURMAN
POWER CLIPPER

Unquestionably the greatest boon introduced into the stable during recent years.

CLIPS A HORSE IN
* HALF-AN-HOUR *
No Singeing required

LEAVES A COAT
* * LIKE SILK * *
NO DANGER OF
BEING KICKED.

Can be driven by Steam, Oil, Gas or Electricity if desired.

7:8

The BURMAN POWER CLIPPER, No. 3, with Wrist Joint.

The blacksmith's work involved much more than shoeing horses. It involved every kind of ironmongery and machinery repair and manufacture. Some blacksmiths even built early motor cars.

7:7 The smith's apprentice. Anon.

7:8 Boys were used to demonstrate a horse-clipping machine on this advertising card. Published by Burman Power Clipper. Posted 1905.

7:9

7:10

7:9 & 10 In every area where hops were grown for the brewing industry, poor urban families would make it a holiday to pick for the hop-growers. Londoners would travel to Kent and families from Birmingham and the Black Country would arrive in Herefordshire and Worcestershire to join local families and gypsies for the month long hop-picking season. The faces in these postcards indicate that there may have been more poverty and resentment than folklore admits. Anon.

7:11

London Types. District Messenger Boy

Æ.a.404.

10513 23 LONDON LIFE. POST OFFICE TELEGRAPH BOY. ROTARY PHOTO. F.C

7:12

7:11 & 12 In the city, favourite postcard characters were those working children that the public actually met, like the Messenger Boy (**7:11**), published by Aristophot Co., 'London Types' No. 404, or the Telegraph Boy (**7:12**). Published by Rotary Photo Co.

7:14

7:13

"TIT-BITS" INSURES YOUR LIFE FOR £1,000.

London Life "PLEASE, A PENNY."

"Oilette"

7:13 & 14 The street musician (**7:13**), or the negligent errand boy (**7:14**), on a famous advertising card, reading his magazine while the cat samples the meat. **7:13** Published by R. Tuck, Oilette, 'London Life' No. 9015. Posted April 1905. **7:14** Published by Tit Bits.

7:15

7:16

7:17

7:15–17   The newspaper boy was an ever popular subject.

7:18

7:19

7:20

7:21

7:18–21 One postcard artist, L.J. Kipper, produced a series of pictures of London child street workers, published by Ernest Nister & Co., which at least conveyed the fact that these children were often very young and that their families were rather desperate for their pitifully small earnings.

7:22

7:23

7:24

7:22 & 23 Another street worker was the 'Orderly Boy', clearing the streets of horse droppings (**7:22**). Published by Photochrome Co., 'London Types'. Posted 1914. He was the equivalent of the Victorian 'crossing sweeper'.

7:24 According to the caption on this card any boy could earn a few pence collecting manure for gardeners, but the written message was contradictory: *This is not quite correct. I happened to have a very successful time at Doncaster on Thursday. 5 out of 7 winners. Not so bad eh!* Published by Bamforth Comic series No. 2813.

7:25

Cold Rolls Aberdale Tinplate Works F.G.B

7:26

7:25 Far beyond the city there were other child workers. This postcard is of boy employees in a Welsh tin-plate works. Published by F.G.B.

7:26 This shows boys sorting stone from coal on the conveyor at Main Colliery, Neath, Glamorgan. Anon.

7:27

7:28

7:28 'Pochin colliers. Just finished work. Look how happy they are,' says the caption as the coal-blackened men and boys emerge into the daylight again. Anon.

7:27 'An anxious time. Pochin colliers leaving train Jan 30 1909.' Men and boys on their way to work the morning shift.

7:29

COAL MINING- TUGGING FROM SPOUT HOLE.

PIT BROW GIRLS, HAYDOCK.

5767

7:30

7:30 Pit brow girls at Haydock.
Women and girls were employed sorting
rock from coal on the screens. The
shawls were to keep the dust out of their
hair. Published by A.J. Evans, Preston,
No. 5767.

7:29 A boy mineworker, from a series
issued by M. Brookes of Pontypridd.

7:31

The "Universal" Pit Disaster at Senghenydd. A Group of Children waiting for news. Benton 138 George St. Glasgow 12.

7:32   Welsh Pit Disaster. A little mother waiting for news. Benton 138 George St. Glasgow 18.

7:31 & 32   Two cards from a series commemorating the disaster at the Universal Colliery at Senghenydd on 14 October 1913. Four hundred and forty men and boys were killed, 205 women were widowed, and 545 children lost their fathers. Of the 43 boys aged eighteen and under who were killed, 10 were aged sixteen, 5 were aged fifteen and 9 were fourteen years old. Published by Benton, 135 George St., Glasgow.

7:33

7:34

7:33 Children at the funeral of three
schoolmates killed in the Clydach Vale
disaster.

7:34 Young strikers, 1910.

7:35

7:36

7:35 The little girl is winding bobbins for the group of elderly lace-makers in Buckinghamshire. Anon. publisher.

7:36 Two fourteen-year-old 'winders' in a West Yorkshire textile mill in 1930. Anon. publisher.

7:37

7:38

7:37   The First World War brought
new jobs for girls among the women
brought into industry through the
shortage of male labour. Anon.

7:38   Women and girls at work in
Joseph Lucas' bakery in Liverpool.
Published by Carbonora, Liverpool.

7:39

Canal, Daventry

7:40

A BIT OF THE BLACK COUNTRY (IV)

7:41

7:39   The postcard age was still the
period when Britain's canals, although
threatened by the railways, were used for
moving heavy goods. Canal-boat families
lived on their narrow boats.

7:40   Canal-boat children lived a hard
and dangerous life. They were kept out
of sight when the School Attendance
Officer or 'Truancy Man' was in view.

7:41   Charlie Flimpy and his family
pause on their journey to Manchester in
Factory Road, Tipton. He operated a 'Fly
Boat' i.e., a fast overnight service
between Birmingham and Runcorn.

7:43

7:44

7:43 Cockle girls pause on their way home from the Llanrhidian Sands with their donkeys laden with the day's catch. Cockles are still harvested here, but the methods have changed. Anon.

7:44 Early daffodils like Soleil d'Or from the Isles of Scilly were big business before the advent of large, heated greenhouses on the mainland made the trade uneconomic. Men and boys usually picked the flowers, which were then packed for market by women and girls. Published by C.J. King, St Mary's. Scilly Isles.

Chapter Eight

CLEANLINESS AND GODLINESS

John Wesley, the founder of the Methodist movement, declared that 'Cleanliness is, indeed, next to Godliness', and the big religious evangelist movements of the nineteenth century were linked to crusades both for public health and for personal cleanliness. Religious enthusiasm had reached its peak by the time of the picture postcard, as had the crusade for a clean water supply that followed periodic outbreaks of cholera and typhoid fever. Big evangelical campaigns attended by huge congregations, including children, were carefully recorded on cards posted to friends by participants, uplifted by the occasion. There was also the phenomenon of child evangelists or boy preachers, easily caricatured on comic cards. Quite a popular topic of picture postcards which could be seen either as sentimental or satirical, was the child at home, preaching to brothers and sisters or to the family pets.

There was rivalry between religious denominations for the souls of children, with important annual events like Easter or Whit Monday processions through the streets, as well as the Sunday school outing, attendance at which had to be earned by regular attendance in the preceding year. Sunday schools were attended by a very large percentage of the child population, and they were washed and dressed in their 'Sunday Best' for this weekly class. Some of the revivalist hymns that were sung, embarrassing today, made a specific connection between cleanliness and godliness. 'Are you washed in the blood of the Lamb?' asked one famous gospel song.

This enthusiasm was not confined to Protestant non-conformism. The novelist Bill Naughton, brought up as a Catholic in Lancashire, explains the importance of the calendar of religious festivals. 'To the Catholic child it offered an annual string of feast-days and celebrations which brought an excitement and purpose to a life lacking incentives.' Young Billy adored the excitement of the rituals and the music of the Church. He would be up at half past five, after fasting, to scrub himself in cold water at the kitchen sink (for his house, like most, had no bathroom) so as to be pure, inside and out, for early Mass.[1]

The procedures of washing and bathing children were a favourite postcard theme. Baby's bath was an appealing subject. The publishers Raphael Tuck produced a popular series 'Knights of the Bath', featuring the universal portable galvanized iron bath. Another topic, endlessly used, was the idea that boys were averse to washing. This was exploited by comic artists as well as by sentimental ones, with pictures of girls acting their allotted role of 'little mothers' in washing the faces of younger brothers, who were known to dislike water.

8:1

The traditional representative of childhood in organized religion is the choir boy.

8:2 The choir outside the church at Bodenham, Herefordshire. Anon. Posted May 1908.

8:1 A Sunday school procession along Station Road, Glais, near Neath. Anon.

8:3 A massed choir festival at Ledbury, 1908. Published by J. Tilley.

8:2

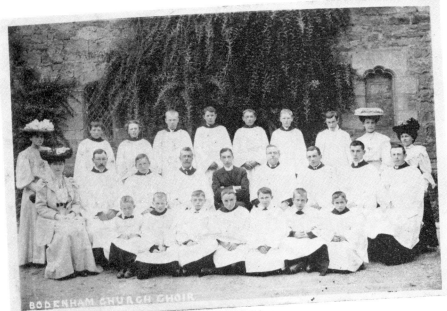

8:3

8:4

Many parts of the country, but especially
the north-west, had big church festivals
for children on Whit Friday and on other
special days of the Christian calendar.
They were the occasion for new clothes
and white dresses. Mothers went to great
lengths to ensure that their children were
scrubbed and beautifully turned out for
these festivities.

8:4 A Catholic procession. Published
by J. Cleworth, 56 Ducie St.,
Greenheys.

8:5

8:6

8:5 & 6 Two more big days in
Lancashire. Both Anon. publisher.

8:7

8:8

8:7–11 Big revivalist campaigns sought 'To Win the Young for Christ', and were rewarded with a spate of child evangelists (**8:9–11**), which the postcard industry treated seriously, frivolously, or sentimentally. **8:9** An unusual small- sized comic postcard. Published by Burrows of Cheltenham. Posted 20 October 1904. **8:8** Published by Abraham, Keswick. **8:11** Published by Wild & Kray, London. Posted 1910.

8:9

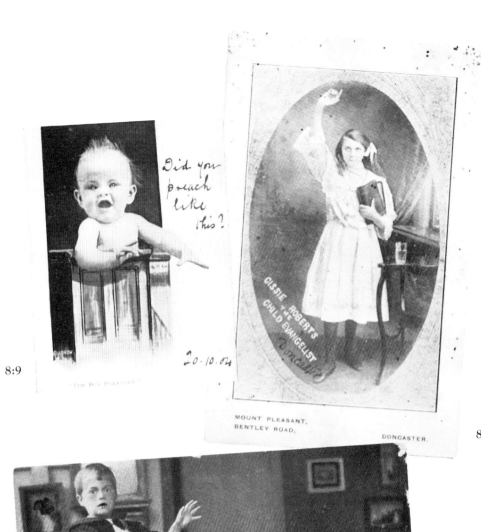

Did you preach like this?

20.10.04

CISSIE ROBERTS THE CHILD EVANGELIST

MOUNT PLEASANT, BENTLEY ROAD,

DONCASTER.

8:10

THE LITTLE MINISTER

8:11

8:12

8:13

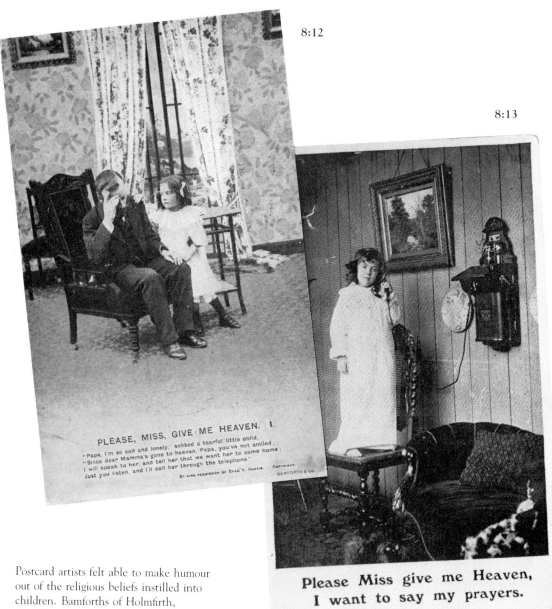

PLEASE, MISS, GIVE ME HEAVEN. 1.
"Papa, I'm so sad and lonely," sobbed a tearful little child,
"Since dear Mamma's gone to heaven, Papa, you've not smiled ;
I will speak to her, and tell her that we want her to come home ;
Just you listen, and I'll call her through the telephone."
BY KIND PERMISSION OF CHAS. K. HARRIS.   COPYRIGHT.
BAMFORTH & CO.

Please Miss give me Heaven,
I want to say my prayers.
494

Postcard artists felt able to make humour
out of the religious beliefs instilled into
children. Bamforths of Holmfirth,
Yorkshire was a firm which began by
making lantern slides of the words of
hymns and songs, suitably illustrated.
They moved into postcards in 1902,
illustrating current ballads and songs,
with one verse on each card.

8:12 & 13 The invention of the
telephone provided new opportunities for
sentimentalizing the simple faith of
children.

8:15

8:14

"Wot's up, Billy?"
"Fader says my big bruvver's gorn to 'Eaven."
"Don't cry: (hopefully) mebbe 'e ain't!"

London Opinion.

'Ere Mister, are you the cove
wot gives kids their names?
'Cos my mother's got two.

8:14 & 15   Postcard cartoonists had a
more robust sense of humour. Published
by Bamforth.

8:17

"I don't see what's the use of washing me neck, if I'm going to wear a collar!"

8:16

8:16 It was well-known that girls were clean, unlike boys! Published by GL Co.

8:17 Donald McGill was the most famous of all comic postcard artists. He drew more than 3,000 over fifty-eight years. Biographers say that he began in 1904 after drawing a funny picture to amuse a nephew in hospital. Published by Inter Art Co., Commique series No. 3500.

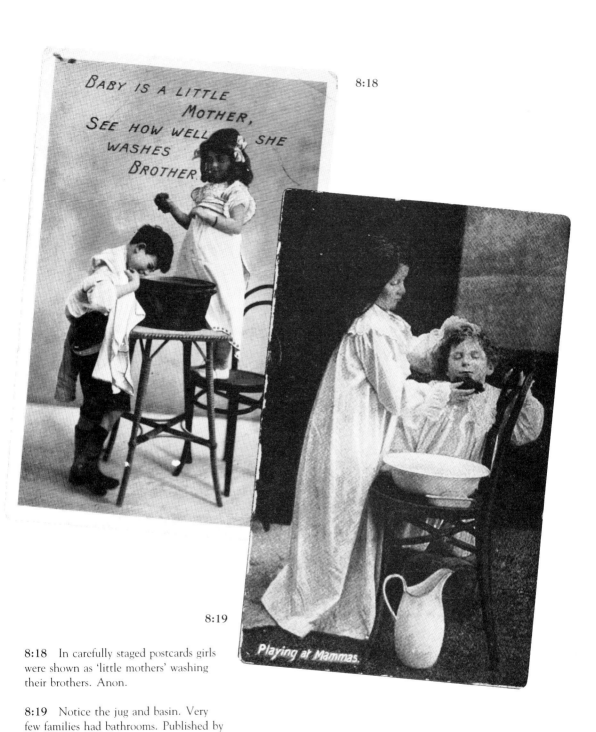

8:18

BABY IS A LITTLE MOTHER, SEE HOW WELL SHE WASHES BROTHER.

8:19

Playing at Mammas.

8:18 In carefully staged postcards girls were shown as 'little mothers' washing their brothers. Anon.

8:19 Notice the jug and basin. Very few families had bathrooms. Published by J.W.B., London, series 301.

BABY'S MORNING BATH.

8:20

Baby's bath was an endlessly popular
postcard scene.

8:20 This example is by ES of London.
Posted in 1906.

8:21

8:22

QUITE READY.

8:21 & 22 These are cards from Raphael Tuck's 'Knights of the Bath' series, sold over many years. Note the ubiquitous galvanized iron bath tub. Pre-war rail travellers would have seen them hung on a hook outside kitchen doors; they were a common sight until the advent of indoor plumbing.

8:23

8:23 Another much-bought card
showed the children warming themselves
by the fire after the evening bath. Anon.

Chapter Nine

PRANKS AND PUNISHMENT

The first decade of this century is remembered as a time when there was no mindless violence on the streets, when parental responsibility was undiminished, authority was respected and the police were loved by all. This is an illusion. It was seen at the time as a period of unprecedented lawlessness.[1] Even so, the disturbing facts of the violence of urban life were not a topic for the postcard artists.

There was an invisible line, only crossed by the burglar with his 'striped vest' and his bag labelled 'Swag', or the convict with shaven head and broad arrows on his overalls, beyond which postcard pictures seldom transgressed. The real world of law-breaking was only suggested by the sins of children, usually boys. But the comic card world is full of boys either anticipating or receiving physical punishment from a stern father or schoolmaster.

So far as the typical family life of the period is concerned, the cards were perpetuating a myth. A famous Edwardian authority on adolescence, Reginald Bray, wrote in 1911 that 'it must not be assumed that all boys become hooligans or criminals, but all do suffer from the want of control and the need of a more disciplined life.'[2] But for most families this did not involve beating. In the 1960s, the historian Paul Thompson interviewed hundreds of men and women born between 1870 and 1906, and found that 'The strictness of Edwardian parents did not necessarily imply abundant physical punishment, as is often believed. It is not true that families in which children were given "a good hiding for the least thing" were common.'[3]

School was different, for all classes. If you read the autobiography of that favourite children's writer Roald Dahl, you are taken aback by the sense of outrage he felt at the brutality of his headmasters. 'I couldn't get over it. I never have got over it', he wrote.[4]

Closer to most people's experience was the policeman. The postcard producers, like everyone else, had a stereotype of 'The Copper' with his helmet, blue uniform and belt. Contact with 'The Law' was, once again, brought down to acceptable proportions by setting it within the bounds of boyish sins. Generations of postcard artists worked their way around the repertoire of themes of boys in trouble with the local, overweight Bobby. They could be pinching apples, fishing without a license, doing handstands on someone's wall, throwing snowballs, breaking people's windows while playing cricket or football, or swimming naked in the pond. Whatever they did was bound to land them in trouble with the representatives of law and order. The School Board man was a similar representative of law and order. Even though the School Boards were abolished in 1902, fifty years later this was still the name people gave to the School Attendance Officer, who was responsible for picking up truants, the market traders on their stall, or those who had just gone fishing.

A few categories of children managed to evade even the 'truancy man'. One was that of circus children (the envy of many an ordinary child), whose parents arranged for out-of-season education in private schools. Another was that of canal-boat children, a category which died out with the death of commercial canal traffic. They lived an arduous and dangerous life, working from infancy, and simply hid in the tiny cabin at the back of the narrow boat when they were in an area where the School Board man might be around. A third was that of gypsy or travelling children. Their life too was seen as romantic and free. It was certainly impenetrable by the official system. It was long after the Second World War that efforts were made to help travelling children with a mobile classroom following *them*.[5]

Through the filter of the picture postcard the sins of the child were confined to sins like riding a bicycle without lights or adequate brakes, or riding with too much light in wartime, or, once bottled milk had arrived, stealing bottles from doorsteps. People sent postcards of such scenes because, in the end, all minor sins could be forgiven, or at least understood.

9:1

"The boys of the Village."

9:2

WAITING FOR A BITE.

The postcard-makers assumed that, left to themselves, boys would always get up to mischief.

9:1 This card holds a hint that boys in groups will 'plot' trouble. Posted in Sheffield in 1907.

9:2 A scene displaying children's indifference to the rights of landowners. Published by Jones & Co., London. Posted 1908.

121

9:3

9:4

9:3 & 4 Two of a vast number of comic cards published by Bamforths of Holmfirth.

9:5

BOYS WILL BE BOYS.

9:5 The same firm issued a number of photographic cards under the title 'Boys will be Boys'. In case you are puzzled, the joke is that the two couples are kissing in the dark as the train goes through a tunnel, so the mischievous boy is having fun at their expense by lighting matches.

9:6

9:7

9:8

The activities of girls were seen differently.

9:6 'Dolly's First Lesson', published in J.W.B's Commercial series. Posted 1910.

9:7 Swings and teddy bears, still a favourite combination. Anon.

9:8 Skipping ropes retained their popularity with little girls for many years. Anon. publisher.

9:9

9:10

9:9 & 10   Posed on the same occasion, girls skip in the road and play ring-a-ring-of-roses. Not activities we would tolerate today on a public highway. Both were posted in 1908. Anon.

9:12

"I'VE GOT AN APPOINTMENT WITH FATHER!"

STUDY

"FOR WHAT I'M ABOUT TO RECEIVE." ROTARY PHOTO. E.C.

9:11

9:11–14 Punishment by Father was an endless topic for comic postcard artists. Punishment of girls was never shown. Maybe they were not as naughty as their brothers. The use of a middle-class setting is interesting as, contrary to popular belief, working-class parents seem to have been less severe than popular myth would indicate. **9:11** H.B. series No. 2164. **9:12** Rotary Photo, 1122b w. **9:13** Published by Thomas Huddesfield, No. 5086. Posted August 1913. **9:14** Published by Inter Art Co., London, 'Chic Kids' series No. 562. Posted July 1920.

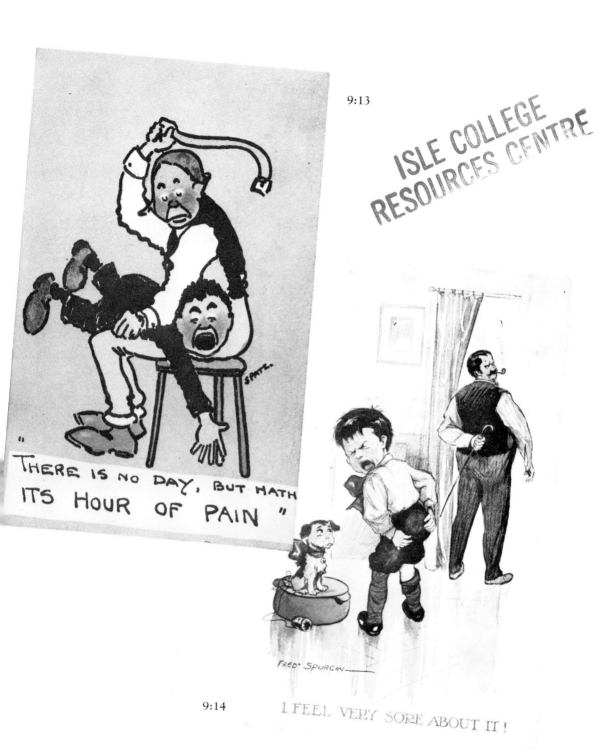

9:13

" THERE IS NO DAY, BUT HATH ITS HOUR OF PAIN "

FRED SPURGIN

9:14

I FEEL VERY SORE ABOUT IT !

A GAME OF PATIENCE.

9:15

9:16   Another variation on the theme.

The boy in trouble with the local policeman was a popular topic.

9:15   Lawson White painted a series of comic pictures depicting various minor sins. This one was published by Lawrence and Jellicoe and posted in 1913. Framed, enlarged reproductions were on sale in Tesco supermarkets in 1990 – a record for the durability of popular image-making.

9:17   We do not know what crime these boys have committed on this card, posted in 1908. Perhaps they were caught playing truant and are being brought back to await a caning or worse. There were Truant Schools and Industrial Schools as well as Reformatory Schools, later renamed Approved Schools, and still later, as Community Homes, to which children could be sent should their 'crime' be deemed to warrant such a step.

128

9:16

9:17

His
First
Offence.
(Tate
Gallery)

Lady
Stanley.

9:18

9:18 Closer to the pathetic realities of juvenile crime than the comic image, was this painting by Dorothy Stanley, wife of the flamboyant explorer H.M. Stanley. She wrote and illustrated a book in the 1890s on *London Street Arabs* and was a champion of the young offender. It was issued as a postcard in 1905. Published by Eyre & Spottiswoode Ltd., Woodbury series 6495.

Chapter Ten

INSTITUTION CHILDREN

The nineteenth century was the age of institutions. For many generations the word 'institution' meant, for the majority of people, one thing:
the Poor Law Union Workhouse, admission to which was a last refuge
and seen as a disgrace, regarded with dread and hatred. There are still
people alive today who were workhouse children and they speak with
bitterness of their experience. It was also the age of the huge lunatic
asylum, from which people seldom emerged, the orphanage, and special
'homes' for crippled children, the deaf and the blind.

In an effort to remove child offenders out of adult prisons industrial
schools, reformatories and truant schools were established. At the turn of
the century more than 100,000 children were in institutional care. We
tend to regard our modern-day experience of broken marriages and
children being taken into the care of local authorities as in some way
exceptional. We forget that high death rates among poor parents a
century ago resulted in far more children being taken into institutional
care. As one sociologist put it, the divorce court has simply taken over
from the undertaker.

Cyril Hayward-Jones, born in 1903, was blind from birth. When he
was five 'the School Board man came round and told my parents I'd got
to go to school and that was that'. Despite the distress caused to his
parents he was taken to the Mount School for the Blind and Deaf near
Stoke-on-Trent, which had a brutal regime. 'The discipline was very
strict: you couldn't talk over meals. One punishment was being sent to
live on the 'deaf side' for a fortnight, and of course the deaf couldn't hear
and we couldn't lip-read so it was a fiendish punishment.'[1]

It was after the Second World War that the Curtis Report on the care
of children reported to the government about an approved school for
junior boys, 'The mealtime behaviour of these boys was one of the most
depressing sights we have seen in any school. Signals were given by the
member of staff in charge to "sit down", "pour tea", "stop pouring tea",

"begin to eat". There was the same sort of excessive regimentation in force as the boys were preparing for physical training. The boys looked strained and unhappy.'[2]

This was the background against which the activities of the reformers have to be judged. Postcards were used to publicize and raise support for bodies like the Sunshine Homes set up by the National Institute for the Blind after the First World War. Long before this, however, Dr Thomas John Barnardo used photography as a propaganda tool to help his work in rescuing destitute children in London who had no home but the street. Every child was photographed 'before' and 'after' and as early as 1874 the organization set up a photographic department at its headquarters in Stepney Causeway, issuing packets of *carte-de-visite* size pictures describing the children who were taken in and taught a trade. Barnardo introduced the founders of the National Children's Home to his photographer, Thomas Barnes of 422 Mile End Road, and the Home also issued cards. 'Also in the 1860s a teacher at Stockport Ragged School commissioned a local photographer to take pictures of each of the teachers and children in the school.'[3]

With the coming of the picture postcard Barnardo's were ready to exploit this new medium for fund-raising. Other children's charities followed, and for many years bodies which sought to provide city children with a holiday by the sea, from the Children's Country Holiday Fund in the early days to Glasgow Corporation in the 1920s, issued picture postcards both to solicit donations and for the children to send home. So did the pioneers of nursery education.

The industrial schools and approved schools, aware of their reputation, as well as orphanages and homes for disabled children, issued postcards to indicate that they were, in fact, striving to provide an education based on that of the public schools, with a strong emphasis on sport, as well as industrial training for skilled employment in factory or field. The emphasis was on the fact that they had undertaken the task of turning the children that society had rejected into citizens. Sometimes it was true.

10:1

10:2

DR. BARNARDO AT WORK IN HIS ROOM AT STEPNEY CAUSEWAY.
(By kind permission of the Editor of "The Sunday Strand.")

10:1 & 2 Long before the postcard era, Dr Barnardo issued packets of photographs to seek support for his work. **10:1** shows his original Woodchopping Brigade. Barnardo boys were later shown at work in the carpenter's, bootmaker's printer's, baker's, wheelwright's and engineer's workshops.

Dr. BARNARDO'S HOMES: THE CHILDREN'S CHURCH, GIRLS' VILLAGE HOMES, BARKINGSIDE.

SOME OF DR. BARNARDO'S MUSICAL BOYS.

10:4

10:3 Barnardo pioneered the 'de-institutionalization' of child care by building his Village Homes at Barkingside in Essex. These comprised individual cottages with house-mothers.

10:4 Barnardo's Musical Boys. What kind of sound came from a band of pipers, drummers, bell-ringers, two mandolins and a guitar?

10:5

BABIES Nº 2. N.O.H. 3.

IN PLAYROOM Nº 2 N.O.H. 18.

10:6

10:5 & 6   Orphaned babies, (**10:5**) in the garden, and well-dressed little girls with their dolls in the bare playroom of the No. 2 National Orphan's Home (**10:6**). Both posted in Bristol in 1912.

The message on **10:6** reads *Dear Mabel, Elijah has been to see these little children so he has sent this card to you to see and he went to the zoo last week and a monkey scratched him on the nose and he is coming home to see you on Sunday.*

10:7

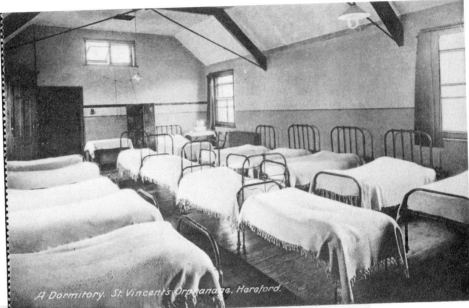

A Dormitory. St Vincent's Orphanage. Hereford.

BEDDINGTON.

take this places for dinner.
Aug 7 1903.

Dining Hall at the Royal Female Orphan Asylum

10:8

In those huge orphanages regimentation was inevitable.

10:7 A dormitory at St Vincent's Orphanage, Hereford.

10:8 Mealtime at the Royal Female Orphan Asylum. Published by French & Co., Wallington. Posted 7 August 1903.

London & South Western Railway Servant's Orphanage. GIRLS AT PLAY.

10:9

National Children's Home
London Branch, Gymnastics in the Boys Playground
No. 12

10:10

Recreation in the playground.

10:9 At the London and South
Western Railway Servant's Orphanage.
Published by Locomotive Publishing Co.

10:10 Gymnastics at the London
branch of the National Children's Home.

10:11 & 12 'Our Waifs and Strays'
(**10:11**). 'Dicing in the Dust' at Standon
Farm, Staffordshire (**10:12**). Both cards
were issued by the Waifs and Strays
Society, now the Church of England
Children's Society, and re-issued by
them.

10:13 Blind children were almost
always institutionalized for specialized
teaching and training.

10:14 A swing-ride for two blind boys.
After the First World War the National
Institute for the Blind founded the
'Sunshine Homes' to provide an
improved approach to the education of
blind children.

10:15 Dr Barnardo's influence in trying
to reduce institutional child care to a
cottage scale, spread to other
organizations. This card was issued by
Sidcup Children's Homes.

10:11

10:12

10:13

REV. W. J. MAYERS (DEPUTATION SECRETARY) WITH A LITTLE
BLIND BOY, 4 YEARS OF AGE, NOW IN DR. BARNARDO'S
HOMES.

10:14

10:15

10:16

ROYAL INSTITUTION FOR THE DEAF & DUMB, DERBY.
Photo. W. R. Roe.

10:16 & 17 If your child was deaf, dumb, blind or crippled, it was taken for granted that he or she would be 'far better off in a home'.

10:17 Part of the message written on the back of this card reads, *Polly took us to this place to see the Blind girls making flowers it is grand only you have to buy a flower.* Published by John Grooms, Crippleage and Flower Girls Mission. Posted Crumlin, 4 June 1914.

10:17

BLIND & CRIPPLED GIRLS AT WORK.

10:18

Industrial Schools and, later, Approved Schools, were for boys who had been in trouble with the law, and for some who had committed no offence, but needed to be in care. They sought to model themselves on the public schools and to provide training for work. Many operated their own farms.

10:18 A relay team at the Desford Industrial School Sports in 1922 pose with their trophy. Published by Heawood of Hinkley, Melton Mowbray and Leicester.

10:19 Boys cutting grass at the Salesian School of Agriculture and Trades, Blaisdon Hall, Glos. The tractor is a 1929 Standard Fordson, built in Ireland. This is one of a set of six publicity cards.

Salesian School of Agriculture and Trades Blaisdon Hall, Glos.

10:19

10:20

Photo by] PLAYGROUND OF THE SOUTHPORT "MARY WILLETT" DAY NURSERY. [W. Rees.

10:21

TEN SHILLINGS

Sent to Rev. R. J. EVANS, M.A.,
20, Memorial Hall, Farringdon Street, London,
: : provides A FORTNIGHT'S HOLIDAY : :
for one such child as these in the Garden of England.

The day nursery movement was a totally different type of institution, which issued postcards for fund-raising purposes.

10:20 The Mary Willett Day Nursery at Southport, provided facilities for the children of 'Excursionists'.

10:21 An appeal for funds to provide country holidays in Kent.

10:22

Willow Street Mission Card.

SOME OF THE CHILDREN AT THE DAY NURSERY.

10:22   An inner London day nursery.

I Wish You
MANY HAPPY RETURNS
of the Day.

I, too, am One Year Old,
and have been protected
against Diphtheria.

HAVE YOU?

10:24

10:23   Paddington Borough Council, London, sent a birthday postcard to each one-year-old in the borough in the 1930s to remind parents of the need for innoculation against diphtheria.

10:24   Children from Newent in Gloucestershire bring bunches of wild daffodils to be put on the train for distribution to London hospitals. 14 April 1930.

Chapter Eleven

BY THE SEA

We usually associate picture postcards with seaside holidays, which most families did not have. Although many employers gave a paid holiday, the pre-war legislation to make this mandatory did not become effective until after the Second World War. The fashion of sea-bathing began as a health cult among the rich, as an alternative to inland spas. The coming of the railways, the widening practice of the free Saturday afternoon, and from 1871 the August Bank Holiday, extended the seaside habit and included the children:

> A day at the seaside became one of the more colourful features of Victorian life, in stark contrast to the drab and harsh routines that marked the rest of the calendar. On Sundays (in the face of strong opposition from sabbatarians) the more fortunate workers and their families brought excursion tickets to Blackpool and Brighton, Scarborough and Southend. At the time of the 1851 census, Brighton was by far the largest of the resorts and the London trains brought 5,000 or more visitors on a sunny day.[1]

Seaside resorts had bathing machines on hire. These were white-painted, wooden sheds on wheels, each with an attendant, which the occupants entered on the beach where they changed into their bathing costumes and were then towed out into the water by a horse. These bathing machines lasted well into the 1930s; they were lampooned on many a comic postcard, and must have been the origin of the beach huts or chalets which still line many a promenade today.

Trippers could not afford to rent them and most seaside towns developed an 'exclusive' end where you would not dream of undressing on the beach and another end, where you could. It was not, however, thought healthy to expose your body to the sun, nor was it thought any cooler to wear fewer clothes. Hats were essential, to protect against sunstroke. Fathers rolled up their trousers and mothers tucked up their voluminous skirts and paddled. There was a little more licence for children. Girls had elaborate bathing-dresses, but it was acceptable in many places for boys to bathe naked. Yet a favourite topic for comic cards was the policeman chasing them for this offence. No historian tells us when buckets-and-spades were first seen as essential equipment for children at the seaside, nor when shrimp-nets and the exploration of rock-pools became part of the ritual.

The seaside boarding house and its formidable landlady have passed into English mythology, and the popularity of holiday camps (which started long before Butlin's first venture) can be seen as a revolt against both.

There was a huge seaside postcard industry. Apart from the endless comic cards, photographers had tents on the beach, and cruised the promenade and amusement parks. Most seaside places had a fishing trade or were close to ancient fishing ports, so local colour was provided by pictures of the Scottish fishergirls gutting the herring at Lowestoft or Yarmouth as they followed the catch down the North Sea, or by the famous pictures by the Whitby photographer Frank Sutcliffe of the boys splashing around in the harbour. That town had other photographers. 'Jacky Ross, for instance was a shipyard worker and amateur photographer. When the yards closed down in 1902 he went into the "postcard trade" professionally. He seems to have had a predeliction not so much for the pretty view as for ordinary people doing things.'[2]

The trip to the coast, whether in Lancashire's Wakes Weeks, when the factories closed and everyone went to Blackpool, or on day trips by excursion train or charabanc, was an automatic occasion for sending cards to friends and relations to say 'Wish you were here' or 'Having a great time'. Apart from 'naughty' postcards, which never went too far in their naughtiness, children had become the natural subject of the card from the seaside.

SEA-SIDE PUZZLE.

To find your Bathing-Machine if you've forgotten the Number.

11:1

146

I'M ENJOYING MYSELF IMMENSELY AT DOUGLAS.

11:3

11:1 A Victorian seaside joke.

11:2 Children by the seaside at Newport, Pembrokeshire in 1908.

11:3 The contrast between the pretty clothes of the young girl and the shawled figure of the old lady leading the donkey at Douglas unconsciously illustrates the enormous difference between rich and poor in Edwardian Britain.

11:4

11:5

11:4   The fateful summer of 1914 was continuously hot. Here at Lancing, photographed by McCarthy Brothers, the whole family got its feet wet.

11:5   Happy days on a Southsea beach. Weighed down with layers of clothing quite unimaginable today, these children enjoy paddling in the sea. Published by Blum & Degen. Posted August 1908.

11:6

11:7

11:6 Mum watches Dad and the children build a sandcastle. No concessions to sun and sand, only the youngest has dared to remove his hat. Anon. publisher.

11:7 A girl enjoys the sand but, of course, she is inside the photographer's seaside studio. Anon. publisher.

11:8

A Lesson in Navigation.

One thing the family did at the seaside was to get novelty postcards of the children.

11:8 A favourite theme was that of the experienced, old fisherman passing on his wisdom to the young. Published by BB, London. Posted 1908.

11:9 Shrimping was another popular theme. This 'Aristophot Real Photo' was posted at Broadstairs in 1908.

11:9

Business before Pleasure: Catching Shrimps for Afternoon Tea.

11:10

11:11

11:10 Two girls in a model car in the studio. Anon.

11:11 A boy in a real one on the beach. Anon.

151

11:12

11:13

Camping (as well as the scouting variety) grew in popularity.

11:12 Two girls in their well-furnished tent. Anon. publisher.

11:13 John Fletcher Dodd founded the Caister Socialist Holiday Camp in Norfolk in 1906. This card comes from the early days. Today it is Ladbroke's Caister Supercentre. Anon. publisher.

11:14 Coventry Co-operative Society had a camp at Voryd in North Wales, during the Coventry Holiday Week in July for many years. Saturday was Sports Day, seen here in 1948. Anon. publisher.

11:15 In the 1930s the big firms like Warner's and Butlin's moved into the holiday camp business. This is Butlin's at Clacton in Essex, soon after its opening in 1938.

11:14

11:15

11:16 Posing in a bathing suit in the
1920s. Anon.

11:17

Don't mind me girls I am only a baby

11:17 And without one in a bathing machine on a joke card, before the First World War. Anon.

11:18

The air here is so strong, it fairly makes you laugh.

11:19

11:18 A seaside idyll from Penzance in 1911, with appropriate beachwear. Published by Aristophot.

11:19 But a 1920s postcard of a natural swimming pool at Langton Maltravers near Weymouth in Dorset shows that there were places where nude bathing was still acceptable. Published by Copeland.

Chapter Twelve

BIG DAYS AND FESTIVALS

In the days before the mass media and the family car, every city, town and village had a series of big events, all eagerly awaited by children. There was the fair, sometimes several throughout the seasons, like the Martinmas hirings, where farm servants, including children were engaged for the year, and celebrations like Plough Monday, when children blacked their faces with soot and demanded pennies, and festivals like Easter and Whitsun. All over Lancashire there was a Walking Day with huge processions of Sunday school children, dressed in white clothes and carrying banners and flowers, led by brass bands. Pamela Horn records how: 'Varying from parish to parish, other dates were kept for events of considerable *local* significance, like the Shrove Tuesday orange throwing at Oving in Buckinghamshire or the rather rougher fun enjoyed by youngsters in Somerset, Devon and Dorset on that day . . . Here it was the custom for the children to go about after dusk, and throw stones against people's doors, by what was considered by them an indefeasible right,' and she tells how, during the Harvest Festival season one village schoolmaster wrote with gentle irony in the school log book, 'This is the fifth thanksgiving the children have left school to attend. Truly we are a thankful people.'[1]

There were enormous celebrations in the cities, like the annual fair on the Town Moor in Newcastle, or the Nottingham Goose Fair, which until 1927 was held in the Market Square in the city centre. Travelling circuses toured the country, as did amusement fairs with helter-skelters, roundabouts with fairground organs, the big dipper and endless side-shows. It was actually Billy Butlin who introduced the dodgem car to Britain in 1928.

Ancient festivals like May Day, with the crowning of a May Queen, also became Labour festivals with big processions led by the elaborate trade union banners, which were also paraded at huge events like the Durham Miners' Gala. Secular feasts like the annual roasting of an ox or

Bonfire Night were intertwined with religious occasions involving children: first communions or the installation of a boy bishop.

Royal celebrations like coronations and jubilees provided excuses for firework displays, demonstrations of loyalty and street parties. Empire Day gave an opportunity for a school holiday and parades by every uniformed organization in the town, juvenile or adult. It was as though there was a hunger for events in a drab world. They were all accompanied by music in the days when few homes had a gramophone and none had a radio.

Children had a big part in all these pageants, parades and festivals. Parents saved and scraped to ensure that there were new dresses or new boots for the big occasions. Girls and boys were at the centre of the stage in the carnival float, the gymnastic display or the annual sports day. Even if they were only spectators they were pushed to the front of the crowd to get a better view.

The postcard photographers seized the opportunities provided by high days and holidays. Their cards were on sale before any picture could appear in the local paper, and if your particular contribution was recorded, or if your children could be identified in the picture, you would certainly buy copies to post to everyone. Winning teams, prize-winners and little local champions were rounded up by the photographer to be immortalized for posterity.

12:1

12:1   Mr Nemo drives a car containing carnival queens and princesses in the 1930 Ross on Wye carnival.

12:2

12:3

Roasting Ox, Stratford.-on-Avon.

12:2 The girls and boys of Helston in Cornwall were dressed all in white for the Furry Dance held there every year in May. Published by A.A. Hawke, Helston.

12:3 An ox roast was held in Stratford-on-Avon in conjunction with the annual Mop Fair. E.H. Tyler photographed the 1910 activities, with several young lads well to the fore.

12:4

12:5

12:4 It was still possible to stop all the traffic for Maypole dancing in the centre of Shipston-on-Stour in 1931. Published by Butt, Bourton-on-the-Water.

12:5 Elsewhere the ceremony was relegated to a park or playground. Published by J.J. Tilley, Ledbury, c. 1911.

12:6

12:6 The local schoolmaster crowns the May Queen at Dorsington, Warwickshire. Posted in 1942, but probably photographed five years earlier. Anon.

12:7 Another May Queen poses with her attendants on the vicarage lawn. Anon.

12:8

Coronation of King George V. and Queen Mary, June 22nd, 1911. Festivities at Ledbury.

EMPIRE DAY, LEISTON 1909

12:9

12:8 Coronation Day, 1911, at Ledbury, Herefordshire. Notice how the children were allowed to spread right across the High Street, beyond the ancient Market House. Unimaginable today! Published by J.J. Tilley.

12:9 Empire Day (24 May), Queen Victoria's birthday, was widely celebrated by schools. Here the children are being addressed at Leiston in Suffolk in 1909. Anon.

12:10

12:11

12:10 The Droylsden Industrial Co-operative Society in Greater Manchester was not going to be outdone by imperialist celebrations. This is its Children's Gala in 1905, where its decorated dray-horses pulled decorated waggon-loads of children around the town. Anon.

12:11 The photographer has mis-spelt Netherton: it is the one near Dudley in Worcestershire. The children have been presented with mugs, so there was probably something to drink. Anon.

12:12

12:13

WAGON CO'S SPORTS.   LADY BRUTON AND FLAG SELLERS

12:12 About seventy men, women and children on a crowded barge wait for the photographer, Dalton, to record the happy moment on a canal near Chorley, Lancashire.

12:13 Many of these special occasions were staged to raise funds for local hospitals. Here Lady Bruton is surrounded by all available women and girls to sell flags at the Gloucester Wagon Company's sports day. Photographed by Pitcher, c. 1910.

Chapter Thirteen

DRESSING-UP AND UNDRESSING

Perhaps the first thing that strikes us about the children of the postcard era is their uncomfortable clothing: not just the poor in their baggy cut-down and handed-down clothes, but those well-dressed children with their boots with endless buttons and laces, the boys' Eton collars with front and back studs, or the endless hooks and eyes on the girls' dresses. Boys' clothes, like those of their fathers, were made of heavy, durable woollen cloth, with woollen vests and drawers underneath. Their breeches came below the knees and their woollen stockings well above them. The introduction of (very long) shorts was one of the achievements of the Scout movement. Sailor suits were advertised by Dickins and Jones, probably correctly, as 'the most comfortable dress for children, suitable for all seasons.' Girls' clothes were even more restricting than those of the boys, for Sundays 'clean, white, starched clothes were the small girls' invariable wear . . . Underwear was, for winter, flannel drawers, woollen gaiters, stays, combinations, but in summer Liberty bodices, vests, cotton drawers, with, all the year round, petticoats. Incidently, at the seaside these children paddled with frocks and petticoats tucked into drawers.'[1]

In poor families clothing was handed down. Pamela Horn provides a picture from 1890 of quite big boys wearing their sister's cast-off clothing. It was, however, normal for boys under five to be dressed in girls clothing. Among the better off the small boy's 'breeching' was 'marked by his first suit made by his father's tailor.'[2] Further down the social scale the event was celebrated by a visit to the photographer for 'before and after' pictures. One postcard shows William Rushton of Bury, Lancashire, aged three in 1920, going in to the photographer's in a dress and petticoat for one picture, and having changed on the premises into a woollen jersey and a pair of shorts, another picture was taken.

The second thing we notice on old photographs is the cult, not only of uniform, but of uniformity. A fascinating comment was made in 1912 by

Arthur Ponsonby:

> Compare a photograph of a group of schoolboys of today with one of only 40 to 50 years ago. In the latter boys will be seen lounging about in different attitudes with a curious variety of costumes. If it is a football eleven they will be in varied and strange garments, with their trousers tucked into their socks, some bareheaded, some with ill-fitting caps and old shrunken shirts, others perhaps neater, but each one individual and distinct. The group today consists of two or three rows of boys beautifully turned out with immaculate, perfectly fitting clothes. In the football eleven each will wear a cap, shirt, shoes, stockings of precisely the same pattern. They stand and sit so that the line of the peaks of their caps, of their folded arms, of their bare knees is mathematically level. And even their faces! . . . Now no one will say that this can be accounted for by the improvement in the tailor's art and an artistic desire for regularity in the photographer. It is an outward and visible sign of the stereotyping and conventionalizing effect of our modern educational system . . . [3]

The third striking feature is the opposite: the adult love of make-believe and the vogue for fancy dress, both in the nationally distributed cards from the big publishers and in the local photographer's output. Some children probably loved it, while others must have been made miserable by the indignity of being obliged to pretend to be someone or something else.

The final paradox is that those over-dressed Edwardian children were undressed for the photographer under a variety of pretexts: bathtime, the imitation of classical art, or a sentimentalization of the raggedness of the poor. Those pre-teen girls, carefully posed in the studio and sent openly through the post raise questions for the knowing modern viewer, but they belong to a photographic tradition begun by the author of *Alice in Wonderland*. You have only to read the messages on the back to see that they were simply seen as delightful or charming. No doubt there were other pictures, not sent openly through the post. But we should not read more into our grandparents' celebration of the age of innocence than they themselves saw in it.

13:1

ISLE COLLEGE
RESOURCES CENTRE

13:1 & 2 The message on the back of this card of this determined child with a hoop explains . . .

13:2

POST CARD.

This space for communication   The address to be written here

STAMP
*
HERE

Dear Mrs Robins you must not go by looks, as this sober looking little boy, is not in the least little bit what he looks, if you could see him at home you would think him the essence of rogueishness, he would just suit Elsie and M.J. I hope you are all well as it leaves us, I remain your sincere friend M A Beard

13:3

13:4

13:5

13:3–6 Dressing up for a carnival or a fancy-dress parade was always popular with children. Local photographers were often on hand to provide a momento in the form of a photographic postcard at a cost of 2d. There was always a ready market among parents and relatives for such souvenirs. **13:3** Published by A.E. Fairweather, Salcombe. **13:4** Published by Dyche, Birmingham.

13:6

1 Dozen Post Cards Price 6ᵈ

"BUBBLES."
By Sir John Millais, Bt., P.R.A.
After the Original in the possession of Messrs. Pears

13:7

13:8

Advertisers were ready to exploit images of childhood.

13:7   The most famous advertising postcard of all, although this advertises postcards as well as soap.

13:8 & 9   Two famous postcards for Fry's chocolate.

13:9

13:10

To modern eyes there is something very strange about the Edwardian picture postcard cult of the ragged, barefoot child, published at a time when the streets were full of real poverty-stricken children who were not nearly so picturesque.

13:10 'I'm so hungry', says the flower girl to the well-dressed girl who gives her a penny.

13:11 'Please give me a copper Sir', asks the crossing-sweeper.

13:12

13:12 Another pretty little girl depicted as a match-seller. Published by Ettlinger.

13:13 & 14 Two more studio portraits of ragged children making a living on the streets; posed in front of a scene depicting wealth and prosperity.

HONEYSUCKLE AND BEE.

LITTLE CHUMS

13:14

WAXLIGHTS?

13:13

SMOKING IS--WELL--I DON'T KNOW!

Poor little chappie.

13:16

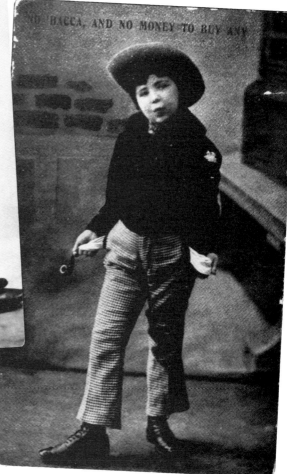

13:15–17 How attitudes change over the years! Today's anti-smoking attitudes prevent child models posing with cigarettes. No such scruples worried Edwardian postcard publishers, who, like everyone else accepted smoking as part of manhood. **13:15** Published by R. Tuck, Art No. 992.

With boy subjects the emphasis was on smoking. *Poor little Chappie!* writes the sender of **13:15**. The barefoot boot boy in **13:16** was published by E.A. Schwerdtlieger & Co., London. Posted in 1912. 'No Bacca, and no money to buy any', complains the well-dressed boy in **13:17**.

13:17

13:18

"OUT OF THE EVERYWHERE INTO HERE" — AN' LOVING IT!

Mary, Mary, quite contrary,
How does your garden grow?
With silver bells and cockle shells,
And pretty maids all in a row!

13:19

13:20

13:18–20   Dozens of artists provided
postcard images of childhood, sent by
adults to children, but collected by
adults. These cards are by Mabel Lucy
Attwell (**13:18**), H.G.C. Marsh (**13:19**)
and Suzanne Cock (**13:20**).

13:21

13:22

"So young, so good, so beautiful, so pure."
Byron.

Photographers too, promoted a particular version of childhood.

13:21 Published by E.A. Schwerdtlieger, London. Posted August 1914.

13:22 Carlton Publishing Co., London, c. 1910.

13:23 The caption on this card indicates the childhood image that the card was intended to convey. Published by Aristophot.

13:23

13:24

13:24 On this Coloured Bromide Studies series, No. 7003, Dorothy wrote to congratulate her sister Vera on passing her exam and said, *I was so taken with these pretty P.C.s that I thought I would send one to you on this great occasion.*

13:25 *I think this is sweet! – don't you,* the sender N. asked Miss O. Platt on this card by Regal Art Publishing Co., London. Posted in 1907.

DROPPED FROM THE CLOUDS.   "Rapco" series 503?

13:25

13:26

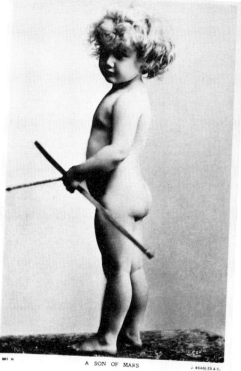

A SON OF MARS

13:27

13:26 Posted to Master Norman Benry of Cambourne in 1906 with the message: *I hope you will like this p.c. to put in your Album as he got a fair, little curly head like yours.*

13:27 'A son of Mars'. Published by J. Beagles.

13:28

13:28 Most of the nationally-distributed postcards in Britain before 1914 were actually printed abroad. But one of the strangest imported crazes was for 'multi-baby' fantasies produced by photo-montage.

They showed crowds of babies being fished out of the river, or coming out of top hats, or hatching from eggs in the farmyard. It is open to interpretation as to what they were intended to depict.

Chapter Fourteen

CHANGING CHILDHOOD

For some people the golden age of the picture postcard ended with the First World War, for others it continued until the second. In a few years' time, if they have not already done so, collectors will discover the postcards of the fifties and sixties. In isolating the theme of childhood from the incredible wealth of visual material that people posted to each other we filter it through the eyes of the producers and purchasers. We may find many of the images grossly sentimental and the humour no longer very funny.

The social historians are at our elbow to point out the truth that 'Most children of the 1980s enjoy rights and privileges which would have been undreamt of at the beginning of the century.' This is why we are rightly sensitive, or should be, to the exceptions in our midst. Today's children have a far better prospect of survival and at any age are taller and heavier than their counterparts earlier in the century. The diet of children above the poverty line used to be full of ingredients now considered to be bad for their health. They were urged to eat up all the fat that they wanted to push to the side of the plate, so that they could proceed to the suet puddings, heavily sprinkled with sugar, and served with 'lashings of cream'.

It is interesting, however, that you seldom see an overweight child on an old postcard. When we asked people about this, it was suggested that this could be accounted for by the fact that children used to walk or run a great deal more than they do today. Rural children walked miles to school and back, and the late Walter Cockle explained that when he was a fourteen-year-old office boy in the City of London, he walked to and from work every day from his parents' home on the Isle of Dogs.

Old postcards do reveal one vital freedom that children once enjoyed and which has been taken away from them: the freedom of the street. The coming of the motor car and the prevailing sense that the driver has priority over other road users, has brought about what we all assume is a horrifying child casualty list. John Adams, a transport geographer from University College, London explains that:

> Since 1922 there has been a 24-fold increase in the number of vehicles on our roads. Most people would agree that the roads have become more dangerous. But the accident statistics tell a different story. In 1922 there were 736 children under the age of 15 killed in road accidents in England and Wales. By 1986 that number had fallen to 358. In recent years, allowing for change in population, the road accident death rate for children has been about half what it was 70 years ago.

This is such an unusual recital of facts that Dr Adams has to rub home the truth it explains, and the testimony of old postcards supports him:

> Should we believe the statistics or the evidence of our senses? Have the roads really become safer, or more dangerous? Clearly they have become more dangerous . . . As the roads have become more dangerous children have been withdrawn from them. And when they are exposed to traffic their levels of vigilance and anxiety are that much higher. Safety through anxiety – if not terror – is the official Department of Transport policy. Its 'one false move and you're dead' campaign is an explicit reminder of the no-go world we have created for our childhood.[1]

We remember dreams of a golden age of childhood with nostalgia, for the evidence is that children were once free to use the street, and that this freedom has been taken away.

Today we regard the period with a sense of nostalgia. Local primary schools celebrate their centenary with a Victorian day, when pupils and teachers dress in long skirts, pinafores, boots, caps and breeches, to look like the scholars recorded in old postcards. The photographer is there to record the occasion, not for new postcards, but for the local paper, parents and grandparents. Specialist publishers for the modern postcard market go to great lengths to dress up children in their version of Edwardian costume, rollicking in wheelbarrows or haywains borrowed from the nearest museum of rural life. Imitation is the sincerest form of flattery, and the fact that modern children can be induced to act out the roles of their innocent predecessors on picture postcards is an indication of the lasting power of these old images.

Those Edwardian children and the people who photographed them, painted them, or lampooned them, have won out in the end.

14:1

14:2

14:1 & 2 A 'Victorian Day' at Clare Middle School, Suffolk in 1990. These are newspaper pictures, not postcards, but the influence of the postcard image of childhood is evident.

14:3 The ultimate triumph of the postcard image of childhood on the British imagination is the success of modern cards using the same themes as Victorian and Edwardian ones. This is No. 16 in the Country Children Collection, photographed by Caroline Arber and published by Athena International, 1989.

14:3

NOTES

INTRODUCTION

1. Inland postage rates for postcards: from 1 October 1870 to 3 June 1918, ½d.; from 3 June 1918 to 13 June 1921, 1d.; from 13 June 1921 to 24 May 1922, 1½d.; from 24 May 1922 to 1 May 1940, 1d.
2. Peter Laslett, *The World We Have Lost* (Methuen, 1976).
3. George Orwell, *Collected Essays, Journalism and Letters* (Secker and Warburg, 1968).
4. George Orwell, *The Road to Wigan Pier* (Gollancz, 1938).
5. Angela Sanders, 'Children on Postcards', *Picture Postcard Annual* (1980).

CHAPTER ONE

1. Some early cards were published with a small-size picture, to be accompanied by a message on one side, with the address occupying the whole of the back, these were known as court cards. From 1900, full-size postcards ($3\frac{1}{2}$ in x $5\frac{1}{2}$ in) came into use. One or two publishers issued 'Midget Cards', half the normal size at a later date.

CHAPTER TWO

1. David Crouch and Colin Ward, *The Allotment* (Faber & Faber, 1988)
2. Thea Thompson, *Edwardian Childhoods* (Routledge & Kegan Paul, 1981).

CHAPTER THREE

1. Philip Gardner, *The Lost Elementary Schools of Victorian England* (Croom Helm, 1984).

2. Ronald Blythe, in Jon Wyand, *Village Schools: A Future for the Past?* (Evans, 1980).
3. Pamel Horn, *The Victorian Country Child* (Alan Sutton, 1985).

CHAPTER FOUR

1. T.C. Smout, *A Century of the Scottish People* (Collins, 1986).
2. Alice Gomme, *Children's Singing Games* (David Nutt, 1894).
3. Norman Douglas, Introduction to the reprint of his 1916 book, *London Street Games* (Dolphin Books, 1931).
4. Iona and Peter Opie, *Children's Games in Street and Playground* (Oxford University Press, 1969).

CHAPTER FIVE

1. John Springhall, *Youth, Empire and Society* (Croom Helm, 1977).
2. Steve Humphries, Joanna Mack and Robert Perks, *A Century of Childhood* (Sidgwick and Jackson, 1988).

CHAPTER SIX

1. John Macnicol, 'The evacuation of schoolchildren', in Harold Smith (ed.), *War and Social Change* (Manchester University Press, 1986).

CHAPTER SEVEN

1. Jim Connell, 'Once upon a time', *Islington History Journal*, spring, 1990.
2. Paul Thompson, *The Edwardians: the Remaking of British Society* (Weidenfeld and Nicolson, 1975).
3. Pamela Horn, *The Victorian and Edwardian Schoolchild* (Alan Sutton, 1989).

CHAPTER EIGHT

1. Bill Naughton, *Saintly Billy: A Catholic Boyhood* (Oxford University Press, 1989).

CHAPTER NINE

1. Geoffrey Pearson, *Hooligans: A History of Respectable Fears,* (Macmillan, 1983).

2. Reginald Bray, *Boy Labour and Apprenticeship* (P.S. King, 1911).
3. Paul Thompson, *The Edwardians: the Remaking of British Society* (Weidenfeld and Nicolson, 1975).
4. Roald Dahl, *Boy* (Jonathan Cape, 1984).
5. Christopher Reiss, *The Education of Travelling Children* (Macmillan, 1975).

CHAPTER TEN

1. Interviewed in Steve Humphries, Joanna Mack and Robert Perks, *A Century of Childhood* (Sidgwick and Jackson, 1988).
2. 'Report of the Care of Children Committee' (HMSO, 1946).
3. Valerie Lloyd, *The Camera and Dr Barnardo*, Booklet to accompany the centenary exhibition at the National Portrait Gallery, 1974, produced at the Barnardo School of Printing, Hertford.

CHAPTER ELEVEN

1. Colin Ward and Dennis Hardy, *Goodnight Campers!* (Mansell, 1986).
2. Peter Frank, 'History and Photographs: Frank Meadow Sutcliffe of Whitby (1853–1941)', *History Workshop Journal*, No. 2, autumn, 1976.

CHAPTER TWELVE

1. Pamela Horn, *The Victorian Country Child* (Alan Sutton, 1985).

CHAPTER THIRTEEN

1. Elizabeth Ewing, *History of Children's Costume* (Batsford, 1977).
2. *Ibid.*
3. Interviewed in Steve Humphries, Joanna Mack and Robert Perks, *A Century of Childhood* (Sidgwick and Jackson, 1988).
4. Arthur Ponsonby, *The Decline of the Aristocracy* (1912), cited by Elizabeth Ewing, *op cit.*

CHAPTER FOURTEEN

1. John Adams, 'State of Play', *Observer Magazine*, 15 April 1990. His views are explained at length in his book. *Transport Planning: Vision and Reality* (Routledge & Kegan Paul, 1981).